CRESCENDO:
AN ASCENT TO VITAL LIVING

Evelyn Johnson & Alan Forsman
with Reji Laberje
Foreword by Debbie C. Blue

formerly released as REGENERATING GENERATIONS

HOW DO CHURCHES ADDRESS THE AGE
WAVE OF TSUNAMI PROPORTIONS?

Published by Nico 11 Publishing & Design
Quantity order requests can be emailed to:
mike@nico11publishing.com

Johnson, Evelyn and Forsman, Alan
Crescendo: An Ascent to Vital Living

Foreword: Debbie C. Blue
Contributing Author: Reji Laberje
Contributing Editors: Marla McKenna
Interior Design: Reji Laberje, Michael Nicloy
Cover Design: Michael Nicloy
Interior Graphics: Reji Laberje
Author photos: Kimberly Laberge

Debbie C. Blue photo courtesy of Debbie C. Blue

ISBN-10: 1945907193
ISBN-13: 978-1945907197

BISAC Codes:
REL109010 Religion/Christian Ministry/Adult
REL095000 Religion/Christian Education/Adult
REL074000 Religion/Christian Ministry/Pastoral Resources

Be well read.

Nico 11 Publishing & Design

www.nico11publishing.com

DEDICATION

This book is dedicated to all those who have rejected the ageist stereotypes and modeled for me vital living all the days of their lives. And, it is also dedicated to my grandchildren who help me stay in touch with the "reality" of a changing world.

~Evelyn

This book is dedicated to all those who modeled for me, and taught me, vital aging through their significant lives.

~Alan

FOREWORD

"You can't teach what you don't know, and you can't lead where you won't go."

This quote I've heard from a variety of folks, but—most profoundly—from a wise elder of my church some years ago. Mother Thompson, in the very autumn of her years but still faithfully teaching Sunday school, would remind those in her class and beyond (through her words, as well as by her example) of the necessity of "walking the talk." Aging was not an issue for Mother Thompson, as she zealously sought ways to continue growing spiritually while helping to lead others in their journeys of being spiritually formed and transformed. There was no diminishment to her life of service to the kingdom because she was aging, but we saw and experienced a steady and faithful CRESCENDO from this precious saint. She was a living testament of Psalm 92:12-14:

> *"The righteous will flourish like a palm tree, they will grow like a cedar of Lebanon; planted in the house of the Lord, they will flourish in the courts of our God. They will still bear fruit in old age, they will stay fresh and green..."*

With joy and excitement, I stepped into the world of "retirement" in 2015, looking forward to this new adventure before me. The culture of the day, however, had already defined this season for me, both in society and in the church. It was a definition I refused to accept. Instead of retired, I now felt re-**fired**! In the language of professional sports, I was now a "free agent," having no commitments that would restrict my actions. I felt that there was more life to live and more ministry to give! I now had more opportunity to do those things that previous time limitations and role responsibilities prevented. "It ain't over till it's over" was a quote (from Yogi Berra) that now meant more to me than ever before.

I also knew that I was not alone. I had joined the ranks of 10,000 Boomers a day who attained that magical age of sixty-five and were entering retirement from every aspect of the world of "work." For those I knew personally, they weren't ready for active engagement in vital living to be over, yet, either.

And so, enter Evelyn Johnson and Alan Forsman, forever trailblazers with prophetic and practical wisdom for the church. What you have in this new and revised edition of "CRESCENDO: An Ascent to Vital Living", previously entitled "Regenerating Generations", are two of my personal friends who are "walking the talk" boldly and passionately. Evelyn and Alan certainly live into this truism. This book comes out of their passion to empower others, to lead others in uncovering and discovering gifts bestowed by the Holy Spirit, gifts that were not rescinded at "retirement" (a word that I firmly believe needs to be retired!). They write from where they live – lifelong learners and committed practitioners. Journeying with them is truly an adventure in vital living! They have not only been colleagues, but also mentors and role models. Most importantly, they are friends – friends who have a valuable message for the church in this important time. Their message is that it's time to mobilize *a living and vibrant resource that becomes more plentiful with each new day.*

To reiterate my endorsement of the first edition: Growing old is not an option. How we do it, is! There aren't two more qualified, experienced and dedicated leaders whose very lives model the premise of "CRESCENDO: An Ascent to Vital Living." They provide historical, theological and practical perspectives on vital living while aging. This is not a book for Boomers only, but one in which all adults, from Millennials and beyond, can thoughtfully and practically engage and put into action.

And now I'm off to my next adventure!

~Debbie C. Blue

TABLE OF CONTENTS

ABOUT THIS BOOK

"Crescendo: An Ascent to Vital Living" was formerly released, in 2016, as "Regenerating Generations – An Adventure in Vital Living".

In January of 2017, the book attained two prestigious honors when it earned the rankings of #1 Bestseller in Adult Ministry and #1 Bestseller in Christian Ministry, both on the book's e-book platform.

In its inaugural release year, Evelyn and Alan continued working in older adult ministries, while introducing the concepts developed in their book to pastors and church leaders. Their learnings were strengthened and expanded through experience and feedback from clergy and laity all over the nation.

Partnering today with the Evangelical Covenant Church, Evelyn and Alan use their teachings, many of which are shared in these pages, as part of the CRESCENDO ministry focused on mobilizing Boomers and older adults as missional disciples all the days of their lives.

INTRODUCTION

We are facing an age wave of tsunami proportions. Approximately 10,000 Boomers have been turning sixty-five each day since 2011, and this trend will continue through 2029. The sixty-five and over population will increase from about fourteen percent of the total population in 2015 to twenty percent in 2030 per the U.S. Census Bureau projections in 2012[1].

It is time for church leaders to envision, plan, and implement *significant* experiences for older adults and those preparing for retirement and beyond.

The retirement age of sixty-five has been a standard across the nation for many years, but things are changing; one size does not fit all. Many people continue to work beyond the traditional retirement age, often due to limited savings. For those born in 1959 and after, full benefits from Social Security are not available now

> IT IS TIME FOR CHURCH LEADERS TO ENVISION, PLAN, AND IMPLEMENT SIGNIFICANT EXPERIENCES FOR OLDER ADULTS AND THOSE PREPARING FOR RETIREMENT AND BEYOND.

---

[1] *Ortman, Jennifer M., Victoria A. Velkoff, and Howard Hogan. "An Aging Nation: The Older Population in the United States." U.S. Census Bureau, May 2014. Web. June 2016.*

until age sixty-seven. Some choose phased retirement while others move onto second careers. Many continue working for the meaning and satisfaction derived from the experience. Many organizations are facing a loss of tribal knowledge within their companies as a result of the exit of aging Boomers, so skilled people are being asked to stay on the job.

A prevailing attitude suggests that being older is mostly about decline. Our society has constructed a system that furthers ageism just as it created and maintained systems that perpetuate racism and sexism.

AGEISM

[EY-JIZ-*UH*M]

NOUN

a tendency to regard older persons as debilitated, unworthy of attention, or unsuitable for employment

(From Dictionary.com)

Although there *are* losses, opportunities to create one's future are possible. In reality, aging begins when we are born. We are aging as much at age seven as we are at age seventy. If we stop aging, we are no longer living. The key question is *How well are we embracing the process of aging at whatever age or stage?*

Another factor that plays into personally embracing aging is the concept of psychological age. We tend to see ourselves younger than we really are. Sometimes, this may be as much as a fifteen-year difference. (Sixty-five is the new fifty!)

Adding to all of these realities is the desire among many to "age in place," or stay in their current living situations, even

4

as needs change. Nearly ninety percent of the sixty-five and older population want to age in place[1].

Aging in place long-term will potentially require in-home assistance. Families and community senior services cannot come close to meeting the needs of the current age wave. In 2013, approximately 34.2 million Americans provided unpaid care to an adult aged fifty or older who needed help with daily activities according to the American Association of Retired Persons (AARP) Public Policy Institute. That number will only increase!

Vital living is a desired outcome for older adults wherever they choose to live, whether in their home, with family or friends, or in a retirement community. Vital living includes a sense of well-being, both physically and emotionally, the freedom to be oneself, and a commitment to carry out one's life purpose. Vital living requires engagement. A community is needed.

The local church is the ideal entity to partner with the aging population, both before and after persons step aside from compensated employment and/or the demands of managing a household. There is a need for effective ministries not just *for* older adults, but also *with*

> VITAL LIVING INCLUDES A SENSE OF WELL-BEING, BOTH PHYSICALLY AND EMOTIONALLY, THE FREEDOM TO BE ONESELF, AND A COMMITMENT TO CARRY OUT ONE'S LIFE PURPOSE.

---

1 AARP Public Policy Institute and National Conference of State Legislatures Research Report, 2011

them and *by* them. It is not merely important to serve older adults, but also to allow them to continue serving. Early planning for later years must be a priority.

Author Paul Tournier, in *"Learn to Grow Old"*, postulated that we should challenge people in their forties and fifties to begin thinking and planning for the next thirty to forty years. Given the increase in life expectancy, that estimate today would be "forty to fifty years." To date, sadly, most churches have not been leaders in meeting this need. Society is setting the pace with the birth of numerous new organizations such as Encore, in addition to a revamped AARP. As children of God and stewards of life, we have a responsibility to join in this movement and become leaders bringing the message of hope that extends beyond this life on earth.

This book is written for local church leaders and those of us who are to assume responsibility in addressing the possibilities for meeting the needs of older adults. We acknowledge that the references to statistics and trends reflect data from within the United States. Although Alaska and Hawaii are included within that data, the reality of diversity in these contexts must be considered in application. The Canadian context is not described within the book, but there are indications of similar trends in Canada, even exceeding percentages quoted for the United States in some areas. Church leaders in Canada are encouraged to access the updates from the Canadian Longitudinal Study on Aging (CLSA) [1]. This study was launched several years ago, as a national, long-term study with an aim to find ways to help

---

[1] *"Canadian Longitudinal Study on Aging."* Web. June 2016.

Canadians live long and live well, and to understand why some age in healthy fashion, while others do not.

"Crescendo: An Ascent to Vital Living" is divided into several parts:

- Part I—an overview of Biblical references to old age, historical reflections on retirement, trends in population projections for older adults, myths related to growing old, critical dimensions of psychological and spiritual preparation for the last phase of adulthood, and stories of persons who are models of vital living
- Part II—a framework for wholistic ministry by, with, and for older adults, a planning process, and starter ministry ideas
- Part III—a compilation of good news stories from pioneers; the input is from leaders with whom we have had direct contact as they engaged in various stages of their process
- Part IV—some final thoughts, resources, and research sites

There is much on the horizon to celebrate, anticipate, and create. *Let's wake up, join these pioneers, and go confidently into the future!*

PART I

PREPARE ONESELF

Uncharted leadership is absolutely dependent on the leader's own ongoing exploration, learning, and transformation.

~"Canoeing the Mountains" Tod Bolsinger

CHAPTER 1

Setting the Stage

What got you here, won't get you there.
~Marshall Goldsmith

*I*s it evolution or revolution?
Which concept best describes the development of retirement and the unfortunate side effect of a marginalized segment of our population today?

Dictionary.com defines retirement: the act of retiring, withdrawing, or leaving; the state of being retired. When one reads the word, "withdrawing," it's hard not to conjure a negative image; it's akin to retreating, or backing down. Who really wants to back down from life? Perhaps this is why retirement was never mentioned in the Bible.

On the contrary, in Biblical times, those referenced as old, advanced in years, full of days, or elderly, continued to live their callings, engaging in whatever ways God directed them in much the same manners as their younger counterparts. Our modern concept of retirement is completely unknown in the Bible.

Throughout God's Word, the aged are cited as resourceful people with valuable gifts to share for the good of everyone.

In Exodus 7:7 (NIV), Moses and Aaron as chosen to lead the Israelites out of Egyptian bondage at the ages of **eighty** and **eighty-three**.

Caleb, who accompanied Joshua to the Promised Land, exclaimed, *"So here I am today, **eighty-five years old!** I am still* *as strong today as the day Moses sent me out; I'm just as vigorous to go out to battle now as I was then."* (Joshua 14:10-11 NIV)

Deborah, the Jewish prophetess known for her Godliness and commitment to mentoring, served as a wise judge for **forty years, well beyond our traditional "retirement" age**. (Judges 4:4-10 NIV)

Zacharias and Elizabeth were both **"advanced in years"** when John the Baptist was born. (Luke 1:7 NIV)

Simeon and Anna bore witness to the Christ child in their **eighties**! (Luke 2:28-38 NIV)

These are only a few of the many references to the benefits and blessings of lifetime service.

If we're honest with ourselves, I doubt many would look to our octogenarians to be leaders in the wilderness, scouts to an unknown land, heads of state, new parents, or even—sadly—reliable witnesses. The Bible didn't discount a person due to the natural process of aging. Although there is reference to infirmities occurring with old age, such as blindness and decreased mobility, none of these issues were noted as interferences with an individual's pursuit of and engagement with God's direction for their lives. When a person was blessed to continue living, the individual assumed it was to be purposeful.

> THE BIBLE DIDN'T DISCOUNT A PERSON DUE TO THE NATURAL PROCESS OF AGING.

~~~~

Secular history has a different story to tell. Longevity of years declined in the early centuries, but—by medieval times—the numbers of the elderly population had increased to a point of reaching critical mass. Older people were everywhere giving advice, trying to help, and often, the real problem, holding onto wealth.

Chancellor Otto Van Bismarck of Germany is credited with the actual introduction of retirement in the 1800s. In 1881, Van Bismarck introduced the concept as a way to help those who could not work productively due to age or incapacity; he noted that they have a right to be provided with care. In 1889 the government approved paying a pension to any nonworking German over the age of seventy, an action that had a very limited consequence financially because few lived beyond seventy-years at that time. Nonetheless, it was an action that brought attention to when old age *begins*. It also established the precedent of a government paying people for growing old – a form of "old age" insurance.

During the same time period, private pension plans began to emerge in the United States with over three hundred reported by 1920. The growth in the number of pension plans was attributed to employers' desire to attract and retain workers, as well as providing a more humane way to remove an older, less productive employee. The German concept of retirement proved most helpful to employers in the United States in the 1890s and early 1900s as the country experienced a shift from an agrarian society to an increasingly industrial society.

When agriculture dominated the economy, there was no stopping an individual until he or she was physically incapable of doing the work. A farmer kept working, often assigning the physically demanding tasks to younger family members or hired hands.

The year 1920 was an historical tipping point in the United States. It was the first time in the country's history that more people were living in cities than in the country. As city factories replaced farms in economic importance, the question emerged as to whether older employees were slowing down production or occupying positions that resulted in increasing unemployment among younger workers.

It seemed that the only way to get the older persons to stop working for pay was to pay them enough to quit working. Thus, the Social Security Act of 1935 was enacted establishing age sixty-five as the "normal" retirement age. This new retirement age and provision of an "old age" insurance was viewed as a matter of caring for the elderly. At the time of the enactment of the 1935 Social Security Act, the actuarial studies showed that sixty-five was an appropriate age and the overall financial implications were manageable. At the time, for those just *born*, sixty was the life expectancy. For those who lived to age sixty-five, they could expect to live another twelve years. Thus, "retirees" were few and they would receive these new Social Security benefits for a minimal time. Plus, of course, they would have contributed to that which they would receive.

The financial expectations of those who initiated and approved the Social Security Act did not prove to be on target. With medical advances and greater attention to wellness, the lifespan of older adults expanded quickly and significantly. Increasingly (though perhaps unrelatable by today's standard), retired people wished they could work. The opposite of work was play, but funding leisure activities seemed to be reserved for those with accumulated wealth.

In the late 1960s the Age Discrimination in Employment Act (ADEA) was enacted to prohibit age discrimination in employment for individuals, but it did not initially apply to individuals over age sixty-five nor did it prohibit mandatory retirement. The evolution of ADEA over the next fifty years became indicative of western societies' extended life expectancies. In 1987, the upper age limit was removed and mandatory provisions were banned, with a few exceptions, such as military members and similar public service functions.

During the same time period that the government was addressing age discrimination (in 1983), the normal retirement age of the Social Security Act was raised from what became the "traditional" sixty-five. There were years of incremental month increases in age until the current provision for full benefits at age sixty-seven for all individuals born after 1959.

Was it too late? After a century, the cultural expectation for leaving the work force was already formed.

Evolution or revolution?

We can say the concept of retirement *evolved* slowly and naturally, yet the reality of revolution is also very much a part of the big picture.

Both the German actions in the late 1880s and the U.S. action in 1935 were rooted in concerns for economic security and care for the elderly combined with a pending crisis of many unemployed young workers. The Social Security Act of

1935[1], in particular, can be cited as **an action to remove older workers with no justifiable reason** other than chronological age.

How have we strayed so far from a biblical beginning, when every person, regardless of age, continued to engage in purposeful living, to an expectation that—at a certain age— we will withdraw and leave?

> HOW HAVE WE STRAYED SO FAR FROM A BIBLICAL BEGINNING, WHEN EVERY PERSON, REGARDLESS OF AGE, CONTINUED TO ENGAGE IN PURPOSEFUL LIVING.....

---

[1] *"Social Security." History. Web. June 2016.*

QUESTIONS FOR REFLECTION

Think for yourself...

What adjectives would you use to describe your current perception of retirement?

Consider the bigger picture...

How did governmental actions help shape attitudes toward old age?

Imagine how it could change...

How can your congregation intentionally respect and honor the process of getting older?

CHAPTER 2

Having Anticipatory Vision

Since we cannot change reality, let us change the eyes which see reality.
~Nikos Kazantzakis

*V*ision is a mental picture of a preferred *future*. Ironically, the construction of vision is most often a past to present based process. It typically engages persons in an assessment of a current reality that is further shaped by past experiences.

Discerning a vision for ministry with the sixty-five and older population of the *future* requires a shift in the visioning approach. We must have strategic anticipation or *anticipatory vision*.

Those who train secret service personnel note that anticipatory vision requires:

1. Seeing the peripheral
2. Seeing the unexpected
3. Identifying the suspicious and unusual activity
4. Imagining possibilities

One of the challenges for the church today is to engage in a strategic *anticipation* of ministry that is needed when the Boomer birth cohort (those born from 1946-1964), becomes a critical mass within the older population. The Boomer's life cycle has, since adolescence, initiated change.

Some of the movements in local church ministry that resulted from their presence included:

- Organized youth ministry, both in local churches and parachurch organizations, as Boomers moved through adolescence
- The contemporary style of worship music and worship teams emerged during Baby Boomer's young adult years
- The type and quality of children's ministry was enhanced, birth through age twelve, as the Baby Boomer cohort became parents

In the best case scenario, Boomers, as a critical mass in the sixty-five and over population in our churches, will transform the approach to "older adult" ministries. In the worst case scenario, they will just ignore these ministries and disengage with the church.

As church leaders create a mental model of this future "older adults" ministry, it's important to identify the potential number and general characteristics of those who might serve and be served. A starting point is to reflect on the current demographics of a congregation.

Consider the Trailing Edge Boomers, born in 1952-1964. Who are they? What are the life transitions they are experiencing? How are they engaged in service?

Next, consider the subgroups within your sixty-five and over population. Various researchers have indicated different levels of aging. The chart below reflects a blending of their theories.

"New" Old	Age 65-69
"Young" Old	Ages 70-74
"Middle" Old	Ages 75-79
Old	Ages 80-84
"Oldest" Old	Ages 85+

Ask yourself:

1. Which age group makes up the greater percentage of your church?
2. What are the characteristics of each of the subgroups?
3. What are the needs of each subgroup?

Your church exists within a community of concern. Each local church has the responsibility of defining the boundaries of that community.

Facts about the population in your community are easily accessible through online and print resources with data from the U.S. Census Bureau. A listing of options for research is available in the resource section at the back of this book. Some of the demographics to consider are: percentages of persons in various age groups, gender, racial, and ethnic backgrounds, marital status, educational level, and median income levels. In addition to reflecting on your local church and community demographics, one should also consider the general trends emerging across the nation.

~~~~

Longevity[1]

The old in the United States are living longer!

- Life expectancy in 1900: forty-seven
- Life expectancy in 2010: seventy-eight
- In 2015, a male turning age sixty-five could expect to live nineteen more years; a female could expect to live twenty-one more years
- In 2015, one out of every four sixty-five year olds was projected to live past the age of ninety; one out of every ten was expected to live past ninety-five

Density

The United States population is getting older!

- The sixty-five and over population is growing by up to 10,000 people a day since the Boomers began turning sixty-five in 2011; this trend will continue through 2029
- The sixty-five and over population is projected to increase from about 14% of the total population in 2015 to 20% in 2030 and more beyond with new statistics coming out every year
- 2056 is the projected tipping point, when the percentage of sixty-five and over population will outnumber those under eighteen; the "new old" will be the Millennials, who begin turning sixty-five in 2046

---

[1] *Ortman, Jennifer M., Victoria A. Velkoff, and Howard Hogan. "An Aging Nation: The Older Population in the United States." U.S. Census Bureau, May 2014. Web. June 2016., Cited statistics under "Longevity," "Density," and "Diversity." Subsections of chapter.*

Diversity

The United States is becoming a plurality nation!

- In 2043, it is projected that the non-Hispanic white population will not be a majority in the total population
- The diversity of the older population (sixty-five and over) by 2060 according to 2012 projections from the 2010 U.S. Census will be:
    - Non-Hispanic white – 56%
    - Hispanic – 21.2%
    - Black – 12.5%
    - Asian – 9%
    - Other races (Native American, Alaskan Native, Pacific Islander and Hawaiian, and more than one race) – 1.3%

Ask yourself:

1. Which of these trends are currently influencing your church and community?
2. Which of these trends may be influences in the future?

With the increasing racial and ethnic diversity of the older population, diverse expectations will shape the nature of eldercare as well as needed services within our churches and communities. African American and Hispanic communities have historically viewed the responsibility of care for the older adults to be a family responsibility, with the younger generations caring for older generations.

The concept of caring for older generations in families has eroded some in recent years, given mobility and the increasing number of low-income households within both of these communities. Mobility, both voluntary and involuntary, has had the side effect, for some, of weakening the family bonds and the sense of neighborhood.

Lower income levels create additional pressures for both those who give and receive care. The option of paying for outside services isn't available to all who need care. Within the Asian and Native American contexts, the traditional assumption is that older relatives are to be cared for by the young, even if children and

> MOBILITY, BOTH VOLUNTARY AND INVOLUNTARY, HAS HAD THE SIDE EFFECT, FOR SOME, OF WEAKENING THE FAMILY BONDS AND THE SENSE OF NEIGHBORHOOD.

grandchildren are living at a distance. Yet, the stresses created by caregiving, both those in close proximity and those at a distance, are becoming more difficult for caregivers to manage. Support for caregivers is now a key issue in many circles.

What does all of this mean for the church? As the late church consultant, Lyle Schaller, once wisely said, "The one thing that you know about the future is that you don't know." Nonetheless, Schaller modeled a practice of mining demographics to engage in strategic anticipatory vision and create innovative models of church ministries for the future.

If we are to take the statistics seriously, we know we are not creating a small tangential ministry for a few older people. **We are visioning and planning for a strategic initiative to connect with the projected largest segment of the population.**

QUESTIONS FOR REFLECTION

Think for yourself...

> What are you personally experiencing in terms of the increasing sixty-five and over population in your community?

Consider the bigger picture...

> What serves as a basis of planning for older adult ministries in your church?

Imagine how it could change...

> How might having strategic anticipation of the "new old" alter your church's approach to older adult ministries?

CHAPTER 3

<u>Preparing For the Future</u>

Old age is like everything else; to make a success of it you have to start young.
~Unknown

*J*ust as it is important to develop plans within a family, workplace, community organization, or church, planning is part of the preparation for the anticipated future in the last phase of life.

The Book of Proverbs has wisdom for here and now, but also for focusing on the future. Many proverbs offer wisdom on how to make plans, why to make them, and what to expect with the best plans we make.

> *Without counsel plans fail, but with many advisers they succeed.*
> *(Proverbs 15:22 ESV)*
> *Commit your work to the Lord, and your plans will be established.*
> *(Proverbs 16:3 ESV)*

Using just these two proverbs—among many addressing how to lay out our futures—we are pointed toward preparing for the future through planning. As Paul Tournier wrote in *"Learn to Grow Old":*

"Your manner of life now is already determining your life in the years of old age. This happens without your realizing it and perhaps you are not giving enough thought to it. Therefore, one must prepare oneself for retirement."

We previously mentioned Caleb from the Book of Joshua in the Bible. At one point while in the Promised Land he exclaimed "So, here I am today, eighty-five years old...." However, Caleb was just forty when he and Joshua returned with their positive words about the Promised Land! What might Caleb have done during those forty-five years between that initial experience and the fulfillment of the promise to occupy his portion of the Promised Land?

The Bible doesn't give us specific information about that time in between, but—based on the outcome, there are some things we can speculate. His faith was strong, so he likely participated in *spiritual growth*. He had followers, so he must have experienced *leadership development*. Caleb was led and led others, so it's probable that he had *mentoring* as both the giver and the receiver. Through all of these efforts, he would have had to *cultivate relationships*.

There are some words that might characterize Caleb; these words can give us a sense of direction in our own preparation efforts.

- **Vision**—Caleb had a clear picture of God's preferred future
- **Vitality**—Caleb possessed energy, vitality, and optimism

- **Vigor**—Caleb maintained his physical health, healthy interactions with others, spiritual disciplines, and perseverance
- **Victory**—Caleb planned, prepared for, and implemented the vision he was given by God. **Forty-five _years_ of planning and preparation went into one _moment_ of promise**

~~~~

As Paul Tournier said, "Start giving thought to preparing."

> CALEB PLANNED, PREPARED FOR, AND IMPLEMENTED THE VISION HE WAS GIVEN BY GOD.

The moment of promise awaits!

ATTITUDE ADJUSTMENT

In 1961, authors Elaine Cumming and Warren Early Henry asserted the "disengagement theory" in their book, *"Growing Old"*. The theory not only claimed that the elderly should systematically withdraw from the social roles of their younger years, due to the inevitability of death; it actually encouraged society at large to mutually recognize that they will one day have to function without those older adults and, therefore, withdrawal is both acceptable and normal.

The disengagement theory was considered invalid in the 1970s and yet the principles within it seem to be influencing many older adults today, as well as continuing to shape the attitudes of younger generations.

The *attitudes* about aging which were formed earlier in life, have the power to shape *expectations* and can ultimately create the *roles* that a person assumes in the last phase of life. Misperceptions of aging tend to form doubts about the ability of the older population to function productively in society.

One's attitudes can shape actions resulting in denial of our own aging process and create barriers that can exclude many older adults from engaging in *the whole of life*.

We need to be reeducated through learning truth rather than accepting myths. Amy Hanson in her book, "*Boomers and Beyond*", identifies common myths about older adults. Some

> THE ATTITUDES ABOUT AGING WHICH WERE FORMED EARLIER IN LIFE, HAVE THE POWER TO SHAPE EXPECTATIONS AND CAN ULTIMATELY CREATE THE ROLES THAT A PERSON ASSUMES IN THE LAST PHASE OF LIFE.

of the myths suggested by her are further described here. They include an inability to adapt to change, an expected loss of memory, a reduced capacity to learn, default increases in spirituality, and a non-societal contributive use of time.

ADAPTABILITY TO CHANGE

It is a myth that older adults are unable to adapt to change.

The truth is that research[1] shows that there is *no* strong correlation between age and our ability to change. Adapting

---

[1] *Andrew J. Martin, Harry Nejad, Susan Colmar and Gregory Arief D. Liem (2012). Adaptability: Conceptual and Empirical Perspectives on Responses to*

to change when older has more to do with how we have dealt with changes earlier in life and whether we have learned to manage transitions effectively.

LOSS OF MEMORY

It is a myth that all older adults experience significant memory loss.

The truth is that studies indicate fewer than fifteen percent of persons sixty-five and older experience significant memory loss[1]. Alzheimer's is a *disease*, not a normal part of the aging process. As one grows older, thinking processes may slow down and it can take longer to retrieve short-term memory. However, memory loss overall is not a characteristic of the normal aging process.

ALZHEIMER'S IS A DISEASE, NOT A NORMAL PART OF THE AGING PROCESS.

Change, Novelty and Uncertainty. Australian Journal of Guidance and Counselling, 22, pp 58-81. doi:10.1017/jgc.2012.8.
[1] *2016 Alzheimer's Disease Facts and Figures, a statistical resource for U.S. data related to Alzheimer's disease, the most common cause of dementia, as well as other dementias, by Alzheimer's Association*

CAPACITY TO LEARN

<u>It is a myth</u> that older adults are unable to learn new information.

<u>The truth</u> is that studies[1] indicate that we can learn and grow until the very end of our lives. Learning environments and motivation must be given special attention. Changes in vision and hearing will require adaptations. Topics addressing felt needs will motivate participation such as using computers and smart phones to stay in touch with grandchildren. Surveys indicate forty-three percent of Americans over age sixty-five are on social media[2].

INCREASED SPIRITUALITY

<u>It is a myth</u> that older adults tend to become more spiritual as they age.

<u>The truth</u> is that results from the Barna study in 2014[3] noted forty-three percent of the total United States population is unchurched and within that group forty-nine percent are Boomers and persons sixty-five and over. The same studies indicate that older adults (born 1945 and earlier) have the greatest percentage in attendance of any age group in church, but attendance may be from habit and

---

[1] *"Brain and Behavior Are Modifiable, Even as We Get Older." Elsevier Connect. Web. June 2016, Cognitive Plasticity, presented by Ursula Staudinger, PhD, Director of the Robert N. Butler Columbia Aging Center at Columbia University.*

[2] *Brenner, Joanna, and Aaron Smith. "72% of Online Adults Are Social Networking Site Users." Pew Research Center Internet Science Tech RSS. Pew Research Center, 05 Aug. 2013. Web. 6 June 2016*

[3] *Reported in "Churchless: Understanding Today's Unchurched and How to Connect with Them," October 1, 2014, by George Barna (Editor), David Kinnaman (Editor).*

not an indication of allowing God's Word to transform their lives (heart and hand). Intentional evangelism and discipleship are needed.

USE OF TIME

It is a myth that older adults want to spend all of their time relaxing and living a life of leisure.

The truth is that older adults, particularly the new old, desire *to make a difference* with their lives. According to a Bureau of Labor Statistics 2014 report[1] on volunteering, volunteers age sixty-five and over noted forty-three percent did their service mainly through or for a religious organization. This is good news for the church and Christian nonprofits **if we can create *meaningful* volunteer opportunities**.

> THE TRUTH IS THAT OLDER ADULTS, PARTICULARLY THE NEW OLD, DESIRE TO MAKE A DIFFERENCE WITH THEIR LIVES.

---

[1] *"Volunteering in 2014: The Economics Daily: U.S. Bureau of Labor Statistics." U.S. Bureau of Labor Statistics. U.S. Bureau of Labor Statistics, n.d. Web. June 2016.*

EXPLORING IDENTITY

A question that emerges often when entering the last phase of life is *Who am I?* The formation of an identity is a key task in the earlier years of one's life, particularly adolescence and early adulthood. The remainder of one's life provides opportunities to confirm that identity through lived experiences.

Sadly, the nature of one's identity often morphs during middle adult years to align with responses to three questions:

1. **What do I do?**
2. **What do I have?**
3. **What do others say about me?**

Prior to the time of disengagement from the workplace, or the demand of managing a household, one's life is often spent pursuing the ultimate *doing goals* as measured in productivity and reward. A question about doing is often the first question when meeting someone new: *What do you do?*

Imagine the awkward silence or the response of, *not much,* that emerges when that question is asked of a person who has retired, whether at sixty-five or later. Silence or such a seemingly innocent response could, even at a subconscious level on the part of the giver and receiver, unintentionally imply a purposeless existence.

The question about what one has, whether asked by others or of oneself, leads to responses often focused on one's assets.

- Investments?
- Savings?

- Checking Accounts?
- Home?
- Furnishings?
- Car?
- Clothes?
- Technological equipment?

The responses can generate further unsettling personal questions such as *Do I have enough?*

The answer to the third question, *What do others say about me?* has considerable power in shaping identity. Who are we when the "doing" attached to the busyness of workplace and family responsibilities is no longer *our* doing and the capacity to increase our "haves" is limited? How will others describe us?

Rather than have one's identity shaped by questions about doing, having, and the thoughts of others, as a Christian, the focus can be on different questions:

1. **"How does God see me?"**
2. **"What is my calling?"**

Ephesians 2:10 (NIV) provides insight to God's vision.

"For we are God's handiwork, created in Christ Jesus to do good works, which God prepared in advance for us to do."

We are God's handiwork, the beloved. As Henri Nouwen noted in his book, *"Life of the Beloved"*:

"....a person should say to oneself, repeatedly, I am the chosen child of God, precious in God's eyes, called the Beloved from all eternity and held safe in an everlasting embrace."

God's intention in one's calling is greater than the products and rewards of an occupation. He has entrusted His people with the welfare of the entire human race. Jesus was a carpenter—it was His occupation, or, what He DID—but His real calling was to redeem the world. As Christians we are to continue Christ's work in the world. There is no chronological age at which we are released from the responsibility of advancing Christ's mission!

CLARIFYING PURPOSE

For a Christian, one's calling will not change at its core during the aging process. What may change is the way in which it is lived out while being attentive to the voice of God and the needs of the world.

Each of us is an experiment of one. We can explore and find the right connection between God's calling, our means of serving, and the world around us. As Fredrick Buechner stated, *"The place God calls you to, is the place where your deep gladness and the world's deep hunger meet."* The person who experiences this alignment between occupation and personal gladness is fortunate. Often, however, the calling is lived out in the discretionary time, outside of the occupational workplace.

The late Max DePree emphasizes this idea in his book, *"Leadership is an Art"*, as he relates the story of his father, CEO at the time, going to visit the family of the just deceased millwright.

> *"My father is the founder of Herman Miller, and much of the value system and impounded energy of the company, a legacy still drawn on today, is part of his contribution. In the furniture industry of the 1920s, the machines of most factories were not run by electric motors, but by pulleys from a central drive shaft. The millwright was the person on whom the entire activity of the operation depended. He was a key person. One day, the millwright died.*
>
> *My father, being a younger manager at the time, did not know what he should do when a key person died, but thought he ought to go visit the family. He went to the house and was invited to join the family in the living room. There was some awkward conversation—the kind with which many of us are familiar.*
>
> *The widow asked my father if it would be all right if she read aloud some poetry. Naturally, he agreed. She went into another room, came back with a*

bound book and for many minutes read selected pieces of beautiful poetry. When she finished, my father commented on how beautiful the poetry was and asked who wrote it. She replied that her husband, the millwright, was the poet.

In the many years since the millwright died, my father and many of us at Herman Miller continue to wonder. Was he a poet who did millwright's work OR was he a millwright who wrote poetry?"

Preparation for the future involves exploring and clarifying purpose. For some, it may mean repurposing. Whether articulated for the first time, or adjusted for a new phase of life, having clarity around one's purpose is a necessary first step to one's future preparations. It is important for the individual to have a clear sense of meaning and purpose. Paul Irving, chair of the Center for the Future of Aging notes studies at the Center[1]. Those studies report that purposeful living correlates with longevity. Having a clear sense of purpose in the later years of life promotes physical well-being and motivation for continued learning and serving. Irving notes that purpose can be a buffer to counter the pain and losses which come with aging. He cites *"Man's Search for Meaning"* in which psychiatrist, Victor Frankl, wrote: "Life is never made unbearable by circumstances, but only by lack of meaning and purpose."

---

[1] Paul Irving, *Purposeful Aging: A Model for a New Life Course*, October 2015, at www.milkeninstitute.org/publications/view/760

LIVING THROUGH TRANSITIONS

Change is an inevitable reality of aging. We have *continual endings* and *numerous new beginnings*. The life we had will not be the same as the life that's in front of us. We must allow God to replace what we've had with new experiences (and sometimes persons) with grateful acknowledgment. As Corrie Ten Boom wrote in *"The Hiding Place"*:

> *"This is what the past is for! Every experience God gives us and every person He puts in our lives is the perfect preparation for the future that only He can see."*

William Bridges, a respected theorist in managing transitions, says that *change* (defined as transformation or modification) is situational, while *transition* (defined as movement or passage from one stage to another) is psychological. Bridges describes three transition stages:

The Endings – a time when people need to let go of the past and process the losses

The Neutral Zone – a time when people discern new possibilities and explore their comfort with the next phase

The New Beginnings – a time when people embrace new experiences and a new "normal" for life

These three stages of transition do not have distinct boundaries. While in the Neutral Zone, the ending has not yet been completed and the new beginning is in process of being formed.

> THESE THREE
> STAGES OF
> TRANSITION DO NOT
> HAVE DISTINCT
> BOUNDARIES.

During the first phase of endings, or processing losses and letting go, it is important to name the real, expected losses. A simple process of reflection and writing down one's perceptions of anticipated loss before such occurs is helpful.

Take a sheet of paper and create three columns with headings:

Things I Will Lose	Things That Will Stay The Same	Things I Will Gain

Just naming the potential losses can prepare one for the actual time when he or she will face a particular loss. Recognizing the things that will stay the same will provide a sense of continuity and stability. Listing things one will gain stimulates feelings of anticipation.

Swiss psychiatrist, Elisabeth Kubler-Ross, introduced the widely accepted five stages of grief after loss including: denial, anger, bargaining, depression and acceptance. These stages of grief may all be experienced as losses and are processed during the Endings. During the process of grieving, though, we must remember that the five stages are not stops on a linear timeline. There may be a recycling of old feelings again and again as we retreat to the past and try to hang on to the familiar.

Transition is a unique time of being caught between memory and hope. The key to living effectively and joyfully through transition is to keep moving toward the new beginning. The Neutral Zone is an in-between time, but it is not merely a waiting room between the past and the future. During this phase of transition, we may experience feelings of disorientation and ambiguity. Questions such as *Who am I?* and *What is my purpose?* should not become barriers, but rather they should serve as platforms for creative exploration.

The Neutral Zone is a time for personal research and development to create the future. We can experiment with new areas for serving, learning, and relationships. This creative approach helps the process of A) discerning purpose in the next phase of life, and B) creating a mental picture of a desired future.

We do not wake up one day and see a digital sign saying *This is the New Beginning.* Instead, during the Neutral Zone— when the endings are still being processed—the new beginning is gradually formed. First, one must have clarity in purpose, then a mental picture envisioned for the future, and lastly a road map created for actual participation in that future.

Throughout the entire process of forming a new beginning, prayer is needed. Yes, we must trust the process, but we must also trust God *in* the process. The new beginning emerges slowly, but at some point it is important to have a symbolic experience that signals the reality of the old being released and the new beginning embraced.

How one is able to manage transitions in earlier years of life often correlates with the ability to adapt to changes and live effectively and joyfully through the transitions in the later stages of life. Many changes occur earlier in life such as: leaving one's childhood home, marriage or the choice to stay single, relocating, moving, having children, adopting, or choosing not to have children, becoming empty nesters, having grandchildren, starting or changing careers, death of close relatives and friends, and other events that require life alterations. Whether it is an involuntary or voluntary change that one experiences, there is a transition time to process endings, as well as create and embrace new beginnings.

Living through transition is like being a trapeze artist. One must let go of the first trapeze bar (endings), fly through the empty space (neutral zone), and then grab hold of the next bar (new beginnings). Flying in emptiness is not a very comfortable place and people often want to rush through this in-between time rather than engage in processing the endings, creative exploration, and risk-taking of new beginnings. Some key principles to remember in the three stages of transition are:

- Offer gratitude to God for the persons and experiences He has provided in the past
- Offer prayers of lament for the crises and difficult experiences
- Express thanksgiving to those who have shared in your journey

- Remind yourself this is a time of reorienting and redefining, not meaningless waiting
- Limit additional changes as much as possible; don't undergo multiple transitions if you have a choice
- Expect to feel some uncomfortable emotions such as fear, anger, or guilt
- Set short-term, achievable goals, so you have a sense of movement forward while you are on the path toward your long-term goals
- Explore your gifts and passions to discern potential engagements in learning, service, and meaningful leisure and social activities
- Cultivate both old and new friendships to recognize your lasting close relationships

During transitions, it is valuable to establish accountability, either through writing and reflecting, or by partnering with a friend or small group to do a regular check-in with regard to progress. Again, staying in the process is key. The more one engages in transition, the more he or she will feel confident in knowing that the trapeze bar on the other side *will* be there.

QUESTIONS FOR REFLECTION

Think about yourself...

What is important to you personally about the topics explored in this chapter?

Attitude adjustment –

Exploring identity –

Clarifying purpose –

Living through transitions -

Consider the bigger picture . . .

What is the next level of thinking you need to do in each of these areas?

Imagine how it could change . . .

Which of these topics, if any, need immediate attention in your church?

CHAPTER 4

<u>Living Vital Lives</u>

The best way to predict the future is to invent it.

~Peter Drucker

We are all aging. Each morning, when one wakes, a person is one day older. The message from Boomers is often that they don't *want* to think about getting older. The exponential increase in anti-aging products and media messages about what constitutes vibrant living validates this message. As a birth cohort, the Boomers have been change agents throughout their lives, creating new approaches for many aspects of life.

The one thing that this large birth cohort in United States history cannot change, though, is the reality that upon waking each morning a person is one day older. What can change, however, are the attitudes we have toward growing older and the approaches we take to live vitally in this next phase of life. Just as the Boomers initiated movements to dismantle sexism and racism, they can initiate the dismantling of ageism. We need these change agents! They can help dispel the myths and counter the negative perceptions of older adults. In doing so, they will help their own generation and generations to follow. They will also help many in their late sixties, seventies, and beyond who reject the ageist stereotypes.

One of the most effective ways to dismantle an ageist system is through increasing awareness of persons who have lived or are living **vital lives** (actively engaged lives of contribution to society through their gifts) all the days of their lives. The power of their stories can help persons unlearn early-formed negative attitudes, relearn expectations, and embrace roles based on new, positive thoughts and actions.

As Winston Churchill stated: "Attitude is a little thing that makes a big difference." How a person thinks and feels in relation to growing old will make a difference in the behaviors exemplified when a person is old. That attitude will be a determiner of whether the last phase of life is "a nonlife or a new life" as author Joan Chittister describes in "*The Gift of Years*." That attitude will determine whether the last phase of life is as full as the earlier phases of life – whether it is a "VITAL LIFE."

~~~~

VitaLives

ISABELLE

Isabelle lived to be 103. Her last twenty-five years were spent as a widow living in a retirement community. That time was the beginning of a new era. Isabelle transitioned from being a long-time pastor's wife to living on her own, albeit in a continuing care retirement community.

- *She started a group which recycled old greeting cards into new ones.*
- *She hosted coffee hours for her section of the campus and co-chaired the all-campus bazaar.*

On Isabelle's 100th birthday, she was headed to the airport in a taxi. The retirement community workers and fellow residents asked, "Are you going by yourself?"

Her reply was simply, "No, there will be a whole plane full of people."

HILDEGARD

Hildegard married for the first time at age sixty-seven, several years after retiring from a public school teaching career. Early in her retirement she discerned that the church leaders had "put her on a shelf." Some of the roles she had assumed just disappeared without her agreement. In response several years later, she commented, "I'm going to come off that shelf and get involved."

Get involved she did!

•   Hildegard continued engagement in teaching and creative arts, both in her church and in her community.

•   She mentored younger leaders until her death at age ninety-five.

•   She was a great eraser of generational divides, reaching out to all generations and using her God-given gifts with all ages.

Hildegard boldly and shamelessly defied ageist stereotypes. The negative generalizations about age would have shelved Hildegard nearly thirty years before she was done giving back. Countless would have lost out on her many contributions.

~~~~

The lessons learned from Isabelle and Hildegard left ripple effects that continue to shape many lives today. The manner in which they lived their lives demonstrates a legacy that, in humility, each would have noted as simply *living out God's call all the days of their lives.*

Isabelle and Hildegard maintained physical and mental well-being all the days of their lives. This is not always the nature of the journey. Aging can bring declines in both physical and cognitive functioning. Life for some just gets harder. Acceptance of these realities is the key to continuing on a path of vital living.

PHIL

Consider the vital life of Phil. Over a period of twenty-two years prior to his death at age eighty-three, Phil experienced many physical changes that reduced his mobility. The onset of these issues led to his retirement at age sixty-one. He then learned new ways to be "at work," tapping into his creativity through painting, counted cross-stitch, and cooking. The products of his "work" became gifts to express his care for others. With the onset of non-treatable macular degeneration, Phil had to adjust, but he didn't stop engaging!

He became more active with cooking and baking, often for large groups. Using a low vision magnifier, he managed household finances, read daily, used word search books, and prepared his memoirs, over 150 *handwritten* pages, as a gift for his children and grandchildren. Through intercessory prayer and presence via phone contact, he continued caring for others.

Phil's acceptance of physical challenges opened the way for vital living all the days of his life.

BOB

Bob had to address acceptance when his wife of sixty-eight years, Muriel, began to show signs of dementia. He was determined to care for her at home and did so for nearly nine years after those early signs. Initially, Bob tried to have her do as much as she could for herself. He took Muriel to church where she was able to sing the hymns and recite the Lord's Prayer. Those outings also provided opportunities for socialization. He extended the efforts of social stimulation by welcoming visitors to their home.

When it came to the point that caring for his wife at home was an impossible task for him to do on his own, they moved *together* into a continuing care retirement community. Muriel was in the skilled nursing area and Bob resided in independent living. He was able to walk and visit her every day and also interact with the other residents. She received excellent care and showed occasional signs of recognition. He stayed active and was pleased to be in such proximity.

Initially, Bob felt some loss at giving up his house and the chores he enjoyed. However, he soon came to enjoy the freedom of his new life, and he was able to find comfort in visiting Muriel, going to church, and interacting with others.

~~~~

Change and related losses will happen to us, as well as to those around us. Acceptance of change releases everything to be

CHANGE AND RELATED LOSSES WILL HAPPEN TO US, AS WELL AS TO THOSE AROUND US.

what it already is and allows the new to emerge for continued vital living.

Finding older adults living VITAL LIVES today is not difficult. Many are within our families, among our work colleagues, in our neighborhoods, in community organizations, and our churches. The stories that follow are a few of the persons who have modeled vital living for us and who, through their lives, have left us with words of wisdom.

~~~~

LENORE

Once the decision was made to retire at age sixty, Lenore engaged in a process that moved swiftly. During a single week, she left her job and colleagues, moved to a new home, and flew to Canada to attend a symposium for a Master of Arts Intercultural Studies (MAIS) program with the North American Institute of Indigenous Theological Studies. Lenore wasn't finishing; she was just beginning! During those years since all of her changes, Lenore has engaged as a part-time graduate student, a commissioner on the Washington State Human Rights Commission, a facilitator of Journey to Mosaic (a reconciliation and justice ministry of her regional conference, Pacific Northwest), and a member of various boards serving both her Native American community and her church.

Lenore cites the two major contributors to maintaining a vital life as: 1) her two *takojas* (Lakota for grandchildren) for whom she is a part-time caregiver, and 2) returning to graduate school to open doors to new seasons of life. She notes the takojas are "life bringers" and the graduate studies respond to her yearning to follow Jesus as a Lakota woman, having almost always been the only Native American in a predominantly white church.

One hope Lenore has for the future is to find ways to apply all that Jesus is forming in her, so that she can help offer new life in the economically depressed neighborhood being served by the church plant she is helping to start.

> . . . FIND WAYS TO APPLY ALL THAT JESUS IS FORMING . . .

Lenore's words of wisdom for those in their fifties and sixties looking toward the next phase of life:

"...plan for retirement and ask Jesus to walk you into it. In my case, the opportunity and timing arose at the prompting of my son's family, and once I said 'yes,' I recognized that all events were falling into place. Watch for the circumstances that Jesus offers to move you along. Retirement is actually life giving!"

WILL

Will recently stepped aside at age sixty-six from full-time employment as a vice president in an engineering firm. He has entered a phased retirement. At this time, Will continues to work full-time as an independent contractor completing some hold over projects. His intent is to decrease time as projects are completed. Will believes his leadership experience and gifts in both independent consulting and related ministry opportunities will contribute to living a vital life in this next phase.

His hope for the future is to continue to lead a productive and relevant life-style that is guided by interests and passions, not limited by professional requirements.

Will's words of wisdom for persons in their fifties and sixties looking toward the next phase of life:

"Work with a financial advisor to be prepared for the next phase. Create and continually update a next phase plan. I used a framework from an article on planning and created my own spreadsheet to identify hopes and dreams for each area of my life."

JIM

Jim looks back at the six years after his decision (at age sixty-four) to step aside from a full-time pastoral role, and he sees how God has used his experiences and education to prepare him for a vital life after retirement. During those six years, Jim embraced an encore career as a spiritual director, offering individual spiritual direction, supervision of spiritual directors, and leadership for retreats. His administrative gifts have been used extensively in his role as coordinator of a regional pastoral spiritual director network, president pro-tem of a newly formed denominational association of spiritual directors, coordinator of *Sustaining Pastoral Excellence* retreats, and co-leader of a local clergy fellowship. Jim has served as adjunct faculty at Mercy Center in the Bay Area for two programs equipping persons to serve as spiritual directors. The freedom to choose how he invests his time has opened the way for more extensive engagement in his community through involvement with a variety of programs focused on improving the lives of children and youth.

Jim cites three major contributors in his preretirement years to preparing for continued vital living including: 1) meetings with a spiritual director which ultimately led to training and practice as a spiritual director, 2) engagement in community service organizations while serving as pastor, and 3) a discovery in his mid-fifties that cycling was the most enjoyable exercise for him which could be continued in retirement.

One hope Jim has for his future is that he can remain open to a healthy rhythm of life (spiritual, physical, intellectual, emotional, and social). He also hopes to continue to grow into whatever new ministries God invites him into and work as a partner in His Kingdom.

Jim's words of wisdom for persons in their fifties and sixties looking toward the next phase of life:

"Prepare during your last years of the full-time occupation for activities full of meaning in your retirement. It may be something new and different than you've done, or it may be a continuation of one or two of the most enjoyable aspects of what you have been doing for years."

SHARON S.

Sharon looks forward to a second encore career in the beginning years of her seventh decade of life. Her first encore career began when she stepped aside from full-time compensated employment at the age of sixty-one. During the ten years since that decision, Sharon completed life and leadership coach training, taught at a nearby university, and developed the curriculum for several leadership courses in their school of professional studies. She also served as the part-time Life Groups pastor at a church plant. Sharon believes completing her bachelor's degree and master's degree as an adult student paved the way for teaching and working with adults in the church and teaching university classes. In addition she notes her connection with the Evangelical Covenant Church nearly forty years ago and related involvements through Christian education ministry in the regional conference have shaped relationships and experiences beyond retirement.

Sharon's primary hope for the future is to continue to use her gifts, be an encourager, and challenge, inspire, and guide those who God leads to her so they recognize and reach their full God-given potential. Sharon also hopes to be more generous with her time, talent, and treasure beyond her full-time working years.

Sharon's words of wisdom for persons in their fifties and sixties looking toward the next phase of life:

"Focus on your strengths; keep learning and growing; let go of habits, patterns, and expectations that aren't serving you well in this season; and trust God in the midst of it all! The best is yet to come! Put relationships first!"

JORGE

Jorge, a scholar and teacher during his career, continues pursuing these passions at age seventy-two. After retiring at age sixty-four as president of *Centro Hispano Estudios Teologicos* (CHET), a theological school for Latinos in California, he and his wife entered an encore career. They prepared for and served as short-term Covenant missionaries for five years in Spain. After concluding service as missionaries and returning to the United States, Jorge continued to teach and preach at churches and retreats, serve as pastoral counselor in his own church, teach at several theological seminaries, and review and update the digitized textbooks and manuals for training of lay pastoral counselors.

These books and manuals are used in several Spanish-speaking countries and in courses at CHET.

Jorge's life experiences and education have all contributed to his post-retirement passions and engagements. His experience also helped him in caring for his wife who has a declining memory. In the future, Jorge's hope is to keep serving his Lord and His people.

Jorge's words of wisdom for persons in their fifties and sixties looking toward the next phase of life:

"Prepare for many changes and adjustments. Be flexible. Keep the joy of your salvation. Demonstrate gratitude and generosity on a daily basis. Have a purpose or project in which you invest your time. Exercise physically as much as possible. Cultivate your relationships with family and friends."

SHARON D.

Since leaving full-time employment at the age of sixty-four, Sharon has engaged in holistic community development work in Cameroon as a Covenant short-term missionary. Currently, she is engaged in community development work through her home church, Oakdale Covenant Church, in Chicago, Illinois. She continues to be a consultant to the leaders she trained in holistic community development in Camaroon and travels to Camaroon twice a year. Sharon believes a major contributor to her approach to post-retirement years was her family's example (persons from four generations) of continuing to "work" after they retired from "real" work. They modeled living with the conviction that while on this earth you have to "pay rent" and help your neighbors. Sharon's dream, now at age seventy-two, is to move to a farm where people living in urban communities can come and learn about the value of the land, the value of collective work, healthy eating, how to cook and preserve foods, and heal from the trauma of life in the urban communities.

Sharon's words of wisdom for persons in their fifties and sixties looking toward the next phase of life:

"Life is not ending--it's just beginning. Dream big dreams."

ALLAN AND JOYCE

Allan and Joyce embraced new beginnings at age sixty when they stepped aside from full-time employment and moved 2100 miles across the country to join in planting a new church. Allan first served as the "interim" business manager for the regional conference of churches, Pacific Southwest, while he and Joyce helped start a new church plant in Santa Barbara. Allan continued to provide excellence in business management for the church plant for over a decade. His financial expertise and ministry focus assisted a local foundation, the regional conference, and two regional Christian camps. Allan credits being a part of the regional conference ministry and working with church plants for redirecting the lives of both he and his wife. This involvement was enhanced with meeting and making friends from many different countries in their new community. A hope for the future expressed by Allan and Joyce, now in their late seventies, is to continue providing enthusiasm and leadership for existing and new innovative programs where they live in Samarkand, a Covenant Retirement Community, in Santa Barbara.

Allan and Joyce's words of wisdom for persons in their fifties and sixties looking toward the next phase of life:

"When the opportunity is there, take advantage and put your whole being into it."

STANLEY

Stanley stepped aside from full-time ministry as a local church pastor when he was seventy-three. During the past five years he has engaged in a wide range of ministries with a new freedom to determine his own daily schedule. Included among those engagements are: serving as a board chair for a foundation seeking to impact the lives of those most in need and a national non-profit board that strengthens local churches by promoting excellence in leadership, consulting for a Christian publishing house, starting his own coaching ministry, serving as an associate trainer with Equip Ministries to train leaders in the Caribbean, taking people on spiritual and educational tours around the world, and being available to mentor younger leaders.

Stanley believes living a vital life in these "retirement" years has been shaped earlier in his life by serving people, continuous learning through reading or travel, and walking with God wherever He leads. He notes being able to say "no, I don't feel like doing that is wonderful" and being free to go or stay is a wonderful liberty that retirement provides. His hope for the future is to be able to stay healthy so he can continue to contribute!

> BEING FREE TO GO OR STAY IS A WONDERFUL LIBERTY THAT RETIREMENT PROVIDES.

Stanley's words of wisdom for persons in their fifties and sixties looking toward the next phase of life:

"Plan what you are going to do when you retire and set in motion what needs to be in place to enjoy that phase of life. It's more than just money!"

PAUL

Paul retired at age sixty-five from service as a denominational president, a role he assumed after many years as a local church pastor. In post-retirement years, his passion to reach the unreached with the Gospel and love for all of God's children intersected with education and experience as he chaired the beginning phases of two foundations for India: The William Carey Heritage Foundation and Truth Seekers International. At the same time he was a lay leader in a new church plant, engaged as a volunteer at a juvenile detention center, and served as an adjunct professor at three seminaries. Paul notes that significant contributors, to his living a vital life, have been a Godly and caring wife, a promising pension plan, good health, and a wealth of great, honest friends in both high and low times. At the age of eighty-two, Paul's hope for his future is to finish well which includes securing the best both spiritually and financially for his family, writing his autobiography, and completing his foundation work as an officer and director.

Paul's words of wisdom for persons in their fifties and sixties looking toward the next phase of life:

"Invest emotionally and physically in serving others—but not as a professional. Make sure you have not blurred the distinction between your office, career, and successes with a joyous and active identity when you step down and 'refire.' Seek to end well with courage, gentleness, and love."

ROD

Rod stepped aside from compensated employment at age eighty-four when he and his wife moved to Covenant Retirement Community in Turlock, California. Although this new season of being apart from employment is only eighteen months, his vital life has not "missed a beat." Rod continues to serve as a preacher and teacher -- providing pulpit supply in his own and surrounding churches, substituting for teachers in Bible classes, and speaking in chapel at the retirement community. In addition he leads workshops at conferences on older adult ministry. He notes that his prior experience in a wide range of ministry responsibilities and periodic changes in location and positions has provided a sense of continuity for his life purpose during this transition. Rod's one hope is to continue ministry through preaching, teaching, and assisting churches with older adult ministries until he dies. During recent years, there have been physical challenges, but Rod's identity as God's child created for His good works provides the motivation to continue "running the race."

Rod's words of wisdom for persons in their fifties and sixties looking toward the next phase of life:

"Plan early for retirement to continue ministry. Set goals for the rest of your life. Plan to move to a Covenant Retirement Community (or similar setting). Make end of life plans."

~~~~

We encourage you to gather your own Vital Life stories. Engage in dialogue with older persons modeling vital living and learn from them.

Recently, in a dialogue with seventy-seven year old Marv, he responded to the question, "What keeps you excited about the future and your calling in ministry?"

"Our pastor encourages us and tells us we're not too old, and we can still take risks and do something for the Kingdom. And I believe that!

I commit myself to prayer, and as I pray for others I feel engaged in what they're doing. I ride my bike with purpose as I want to be ready physically if and when He may open the door for me to be in active ministry again.

I keep in touch with key people I've had a relationship with for years. These "Young Lions of Judah" make me feel strong as I watch and listen and pray for them as they work in the Kingdom.

I read and journal and pray, sometimes almost as an exercise of discipline, but I press on. And at times there comes a light of Joy!

And when a possibility for further engagement in direct ministry comes along I make myself available.

The adventure of following Him goes on! Even at seventy-seven, I like it!"

Marv's adventure does continue to go on and on as, not long after he spoke these words, he accepted an interim position as pastor of an international ministry in Hong Kong.

~~~~

The vitality of older persons is not a recent phenomenon. Some of the greatest achievers in recent centuries were older persons engaged in vital living. When accomplishments big and small are recognized without regard for assignment to age, we—as a society—can begin the work of removing our expectations of limitations.

- Nelson Mandela, at age seventy-six, was elected president of South Africa
- Mother Theresa established the "Missionaries of Charity" order of nuns when she was forty and was awarded the Nobel Peace Prize when she was sixty-nine
- Anna Mary (Grandma) Robertson Moses first picked up a paintbrush when she was seventy-six, but her paintings are sensations in New York, Vienna, and Paris

Hope is stronger than memory.

Now faith is being sure of what we hope for and certain of what we do not see.

(Hebrews 11:1 NIV)

Hope as a noun is an attitude of the mind based upon the expectation of positive outcomes. Hope as a verb is to expect with confidence.

Hope is the very conviction that led Hildegard to "come off the shelf" despite what those around her were subtly communicating. She accepted the reality of change, transitioned effectively, and initiated new beginnings for a life of significance during her remaining twenty-eight years. It's a life of significance that emerges from each of these Vital Life stories.

QUESTIONS FOR REFLECTION

Think about yourself...

> What learnings have you gained from the vital lives of older adults in your life?

Consider the bigger picture...

> Who are the older adults living vital lives with whom you interact today? What are you learning?

Imagine how it could change...

> How can your church highlight the stories of their older adults living vital lives?

IN SUMMARY....

Ageism is another "ism" such as sexism and racism that continues to infiltrate our society and even our churches. A looming factor here is that ageism can be externally imposed or may be a product of one's own denial. As with any "ism" personal experience and relationships are necessary to overcome faulty perceptions.

The Bible speaks of our journey with God not ending here on earth until we draw our last breath. Living fully until we die is God's plan for our lives. There are numerous scriptures depicting the benefits of growing old and staying faithful.

> LIVING FULLY UNTIL WE DIE IS GOD'S PLAN FOR OUR LIVES.

Recently someone said, and it has probably been said many times, that getting older can be difficult, but dying young is a poor alternative. Even though there are often burdens involved in the aging process, there is also the opportunity to make choices about generous living and giving and there are some amazing benefits to aging:

- There is accumulated wisdom
- There may be resources to share
- There is time to give
- Mentoring opportunities abound

It is clear that getting older is a process. Most people have experienced childhood and adolescence. Many have also seen life as a young or middle-aged adult; but, many of you have not been old.

A large number of people are experiencing later years and increasing numbers are on the precipice of those experiences. In order for the later years of life to be significant, planning, preparation, and practice are required. These ideas have all been mentioned.

What has to be reiterated is that one size does not fit all. There is no single right way. Each person approaches aging differently. Each congregation should tailor ministry by, with, and for older adults based on their own internal and external demographics.

According to gerontologists, sociologists and psychologists there are many stages of aging, including:

- New old
- Young old
- Middle old
- Old
- Oldest old

Each stage of aging will have differing wants, needs, and interests.

The same principle runs as a thread through the many cultures in our increasingly diverse country. The challenges of maintaining the worth and dignity of all, regardless of age, are common. Perceptions of the responsibility for caring for older adults do have variances among African American, Asian, Hispanic, Native American, Alaskan Native, Hawaiian Native, Pacific Islander, and White communities. We can learn from one another.

The overarching concept presented in the preparation guide provided here (and lived through so many vital life stories shared) is that we must raise awareness. We have to define reality. The changing demographics are influencing our society and affecting our churches. It is a new day and the characteristics of older adults will continue to change. Ministry by, with and for an aging population is more than potlucks and personal care. It is about valuing and celebrating life. It is about what God can do through committed people. Churches have the opportunity to lead the way and not default by reacting.

God can and will use us at any age. There is no age limit on the way He works. The time is right and the need is great to continue serving God by honoring, encouraging, preparing and equipping God's people to love and serve the body of Christ and the communities around us. This applies to people of all ages and especially for those whom God has gifted with longevity.

PART II
PLAN TO SERVE OTHERS

Enough talk. Now, let's make a difference in someone else's life today. Let's go serve somebody.

~Dave Workman

CHAPTER 5

A Framework for Planning

Old age is not old until regrets take the place of dreams.

~Unknown

*Y*ou *can* do anything, but you *can't* do everything. Making wise choices for investment of resources—specifically time and money—is essential in planning older adult ministries. The desired outcome of those ministries is to further the ongoing growth of older adults to be like the tree described in Psalm 1:3 (NIV).

> *That person is like a tree planted by streams of water, which yields its fruit in season and whose leaf does not wither—whatever they do prospers.*

It is the sum of all we do that matters. The past influences the present, which helps us to prepare for the future. We often talk about the quantity of life – a number that, as we've addressed, has significantly increased over the past century, but we fail to talk about the quality of life. How do we help people enhance the quality of life when they are at the crossroads of what has ended and what is yet to come?

> THE PAST INFLUENCES THE
> PRESENT, WHICH HELPS US
> TO PREPARE FOR THE
> FUTURE.

The acrostic SPICES provides us with a framework for planning as we envision ministries for persons in their pre-retirement and retirement years. Spices are referenced frequently in the Bible. They enhance flavor, provide fragrance and sometimes are part of soothing balms. Spices grow on plants and trees. Often every part of the plant is used: leaves, branches, bark, blossoms and roots. This wholistic picture depicts our approach to encouraging significant, vital living all the days of our lives.

S.PICES

S = SPIRITUAL

Spirituality is the core of our being. We need to become who God called us to be, heeding the Apostle Paul's words:

> *But one thing I do: Forgetting what is behind and straining toward what is ahead, I press on toward the goal to win the prize for which God has called me heavenward in Christ Jesus.*
>
> *(Philippians 3:13b-14 NIV)*

If we imagine a circle with God as the center, we do not want to stay on the circumference of the circle! We must move toward the center and ultimately live out of it. We are not to be nomadic wanderers in this life; God wants us to be journeyers who are intentionally moving toward the center, our home with Him. As Henri Nouwen suggests in *"Lifesigns"*:

Home is the place where we do not have to be afraid.
Home is the place where we can let our defenses down.
Home is the place where we can be free.
Home is the place where we can laugh and cry.
Home is where complete joy can be known.

The SPIRITUAL component of vital living is foundational to our ministry.

We must be intentional in introducing persons to Jesus and inviting them to follow Him. There are many Boomers and older adults who have not heard the message and/or have not made the choice of a personal relationship with Jesus.

A wide variety of experiences is needed to stimulate growth in discipleship among Boomers and older adults. The spiritual journey is just that --- a journey with seasons and, as experienced in our environment, seasons repeat but are different. As described by Adele Calhoun in the *Spiritual Disciplines Handbook*[1], the choice of a fruitful approach to stimulate growth will relate to discernment of one's current season.

---

[1] *Calhoun, Adele Ahlberg.* Spiritual Disciplines Handbook: Practices That Transform Us. *IVP Books, an Imprint of InterVarsity Press, 2015.*

sP.ICES

P=PHYSICAL

We are fearfully and wonderfully made. Scripture describes our need to care for the body, the temple of the Holy Spirit. Regular physical activity is essential to maintain one's health and well- being. "Regular" is the operative word. In the book, *"Outliers"*, author, Malcolm Gladwell, says that it takes roughly 10,000 hours of practice to achieve mastery in a field. That concept can be applied to physical exercise, as much as to other habits. Practice doesn't necessarily make perfect, but it does make a difference. Yes, as we age, physical activity does get harder, but there are adaptations such as exercises while sitting on a chair, including yoga. Taking a good thirty-minute walk, no matter what the speed, is helpful every day. Strength and stamina can be maintained and even increased regardless of age.

Other important "to dos" which enhance physical well-being include proper sleep, nutrition, and regular check-ups with doctors and a dentist. An additional dimension that deserves attention is fall prevention. Older persons should set realistic goals to increase activity, change their environments to reduce the risk factors associated with falling, and exercise to increase strength and balance.

Indirect aspects of physical well- being that need to be considered include accessible housing, end of life decision making, and overall financial health. Yes, there are many secular services in the community that can be accessed for these services, but the benefits of guidance being provided by a person with a Christian perspective cannot be underestimated.

SP**I.**CES

I=INTELLECTUAL

We have a mind—a brain capable of thought—and, contrary to what many believe, our brain cells keep growing. Intellectual wellness should be fostered in much the same way as one's physical wellness. Opportunities can be created to help people maintain engagement in creative and stimulating mental activities, expand their knowledge bases, and use multiple resources to learn more about the world around them. The growth mindset interventions developed by Carol Dweck of Stanford University are being applied primarily to adolescents and college students. Yet, she has noted that they could readily be adapted for working with mid-life and older adults to address issues of memory loss and cognitive decline. Again, this is a signal of the importance of replacing the *myths* about old age with *truths* in order to avoid fixed mindsets.

All persons, regardless of age, can continue to stimulate brain activity by engaging in activities that challenge and expand the thought processes. There are benefits beyond the entertainment of watching quiz shows like *Jeopardy*. These types of shows provide opportunities for recall in answering questions.

Other activities also valuable in intellectual stimulation include:

- Playing strategy board or computer games
- Doing crossroad puzzles
- Completing word searches

We can add to that list a variety of means for expanding knowledge through reading, watching documentaries, listening to TED talks, attending lectures, and even enrolling in college courses or continuing education offerings. *NetWellness,* associated with the University of Ohio, has reported that two decades of research indicates that *"healthy older brains are often as good as or better than younger brains in a wide variety of tasks."*

SPI**C.**ES

C=COMMUNITY

The early Christians in Acts ate together, encouraged one another, prayed together, studied together, worshipped together and gave to anyone who had need. They were a community and had favor in the larger community. The biblical word describing this community is koinonia. It is deeper than fellowship or social experiences. It is about mutual participation, transparency, unity, and interdependence.

Experiencing community is critical to vital, joy-filled living. In 2016 Harvard Medical School professor and researcher, Robert Waldinger, reported[1] on a seventy-five year ongoing study of Harvard Medical School with 724 men. Eighty of the men are now in their nineties. **The major finding of the study was that the key to happiness is good relationships, regardless of socioeconomic status.** Although the study focused on males, there is circumstantial evidence that the same findings hold true for females.

Planning for nurturing relationships is deciding to build a BRIDGE to connect to the world around you.

- **B**e welcoming to new people
- **R**eceive input and learn from people of different ages, races, socioeconomic level, geographical areas, and faith traditions
- **I**nitiate common interest groups in your circles of influence
- **D**evelop closer relationships with family and long-term friends
- **G**row closer in relationships while grieving the losses of moves, illnesses, and death (create new beginnings)
- **E**xpand connections outside of your existing community to enlarge your sphere of care

Creating community must be an intentional undertaking. Attention needs to be given to moving beyond the pseudo-community to the true community as described

> CREATING COMMUNITY MUST BE AN INTENTIONAL UNDERTAKING.

by Scott Peck in The Different Drum. This means learning how to communicate honestly with each other which requires

---

[1] *"What Makes a Good Life? Lessons from the Longest Study on Happiness"* *Robert Waldinger: Harvard University, Web. 2016.*

transparency and vulnerability. There must be a commitment to "be with other" in times of joy and sorrow, to empathize regardless of the human condition. Conflict is resolved in a healthy, God honoring process. True community is inclusive. Exclusivity is its enemy. The spirit of this true community is a spirit of peace and love. It is the spirit of Jesus - Father, Son, and Holy Spirit.

SPIC**E**.S

E = EMOTIONAL

Rejoice with each other, weep together, encourage each other, live in harmony with one another, do good to all, especially those in the household of faith. These reminders found in Romans 12 and other Biblical references support emotional well-being.

In his book, *"Childhood and Society,"* Erik Erikson discusses the balancing of extremes in each of life's stages. It is not that one side wins, but rather that the tension is maintained between the extremes.

- A small child wrestles between trust and mistrust
- For the adolescent, there is a struggle between identity and role confusion
- Middle-aged persons have tension between generativity and self-absorption

Middle-age is when preparation should begin for the next phase of life. How the extremes balance in this stage could adversely affect maintaining the tensions with old age. The tendency of many in middle age is to become self-absorbed and isolated, which leads to stagnation. Generativity points, however, to being other oriented, often through grandparenting, socializing with friends, or engaging in some form of volunteer work.

The eighth stage, per Erikson's theory, is "old age," during which the task at hand is to balance the extremes of integrity and despair. Integrity implies acceptance of a life well-lived, acknowledging regrets, but not dwelling on them. Despair is a lack of future hope and a sense of not having lived a full and meaningful life. In despair, one gets buried in his or her regrets.

In Erikson's last book, "*The Life Cycle Completed*", his wife, Joan, added a "ninth stage" for the oldest old. She simply noted that in this stage when increased difficulties emerge, the wise course of action is to face down despair with faith and appropriate humility.

Whatever the stage, middle-age to the oldest old, emotional well-being needs to be cultivated. It can make a difference in the capacity for accepting one's feelings and enjoying life despite the disappointments and frustrations.

SPICE**S.**

S = SERVICE

Serving others is not optional for the Christian; it is a way of life. It is a matter of obedience to serve following the model of Jesus. The only option is the choice of where, who, and how much time to invest in serving.

In a recent study by Age Wave cited in the Wall Street Journal [1] , the findings noted two-thirds of the retirees responding noted that retirement is the best time in life to give back their time, talent, and money. When the researchers explored this finding, they discovered older adults are three times more likely to cite greater happiness being related to helping people in need as compared to spending money on themselves. The retirees that volunteered or donated noted a stronger sense of purpose than those that did not volunteer or donate. This research confirmed results of a survey several years ago by Encore, a nonprofit organization committed to engaging Boomers and older adults in mission with a purpose. In the Encore survey 87 percent of older respondents said they felt a responsibility to help those less fortunate than themselves, and 70 percent said that it was important to leave the world a better place.

For a Christian, the gift of years allows one to continue and often increase contributing to the work of building the kingdom of God here on earth. The participation is both within the church community as well as externally through the church's ministries or other organizations in the broader local, regional, and global community.

Regardless of our life stage we are called to intentionally engage in God's mission. The pathway is given in Micah 6:8: *"He has shown you, O mortal, what is good. And what does the Lord require of you? To act justly and to love mercy and to walk humbly with your God."*

---

1   Lourosa, Cristina. "The Top 5 Retirement Posts of 2016 from the WSJ's Experts Blog – At A Glance." The Wall Street Journal, Dow Jones & Company, 18 Jan. 2017, blogs.wsj.com/briefly/2017/01/18/the-top-5-retirement-posts-of-2016-from-the-wsjs-experts-blog-at-a-glance/.

QUESTIONS FOR REFLECTION

Think for yourself... How are you personally pursuing growth in each of the dimensions of SPICES?

SPIRITUAL?

PHYSICAL?

INTELLECTUAL?

COMMUNITY?

EMOTIONAL?

SERVICE?

Consider the bigger picture... What current ministries in your church address each of the SPICES dimensions?

SPIRITUAL?

PHYSICAL?

INTELLECTUAL?

COMMUNITY?

EMOTIONAL?

SERVICE?

Imagine how it could change . . . What ministries by, with, and for older adults and pre-retirees need to be continued and strengthened? Started? Stopped?

CHAPTER 6

From Vision to Action

Do not go where the path may lead, go instead where there is no path and leave a trail.

~Ralph Waldo Emerson

*P*lanning ministries to serve the evolving interests and needs of the "new old" (Boomers who have been turning sixty-five since 2011) and those who are seventy plus, many of whom reject the ageist stereotypes, is uncharted territory. It is critical in the planning process to have a guide and a map with signposts noting "places to visit" along the way. The guide is a leadership team of persons who are passionate about helping persons experience vital living all the days of their lives.

CREATING AND EQUIPPING THE TEAM

Experience has shown that a well-developed ministry leadership team is necessary for an older adult ministry to get traction and flourish. In situations where a strong team is not in place, the ministry is likely to sputter and not flourish.

A team should include five to nine persons representing a broad age spectrum from fifty to age eighty-five and over. Primary characteristics to be sought in the team members, in addition to passion and sense of call to this area of ministry, include:

- A personal modeling of purposeful living
- Capacity to create a mental picture of a desired future
- Organizational skills to develop implementation plans
- The ability to inspire others to act

Once a team is recruited, it is critical to engage in the team-building process as well as equip them for the task. Team building includes experiences that help the members grow in understanding: a) their purpose, b) the context of those they will serve, c) other members within the team, and d) themselves. Even after an initial intensive focus on team building, it is highly recommended that each meeting of the team include a short time focused on team building.

The initial equipping of a team can best be accomplished through a three- to four-hour learning experience that includes explorations of a number of topics relevant to the older adult ministries. A basic session outline could include the following:

- Biblical insights for later years of life
- History of retirement as an "official" part of life
- Myths and realities of aging today
- Demographic trends both inside and outside the church's community
- Framework for a wholistic ministry by, with, and for older adults
- Starter ministry ideas

A summary of forming a leadership team for this ministry is given in Appendix A at the back of the book.

GATHERING BACKGROUND INFORMATION

The next step in the team's planning process is two-fold. First, it is necessary to gather specific demographic information for the individual church context, as well as for the community served by the church. Second, it's important to solicit the thoughts and feelings among those within the existing Baby Boomer and sixty-five and over constituency via focus groups and surveys. The themes within the results of this data gathered, by either the entire team or subgroups within the team, can provide a backdrop to engage in the visioning process for the future.

USE BACKGROUND INFORMATION TO PROVIDE A BACKDROP TO ENGAGE IN THE VISIONING PROCESS FOR THE FUTURE.

VISION TO ACTION

Signposts noting "places to visit" along the journey are vital to staying on track. The first signpost is at the beginning of the journey – prayer. It is God's direction that you are discerning for a particular place with a particular people at a particular time.

> *Ask and it will be given to you; seek and you will find; knock and the door will be opened to you.*
>
> *(Matthew 7:7 NIV)*

Prayer continues as you visit the other places along the way and throughout the implementation. After initiating prayer, there are 4 Ps as suggested by William Bridges in the preparing for a new beginning.

Prayer: What are the specific areas for prayer focus? As a team? As a church? As an individual?

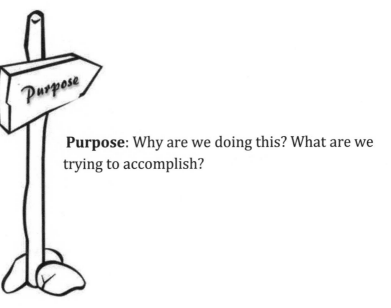

Purpose: Why are we doing this? What are we trying to accomplish?

Picture: What is the end result? How is it going   to work?

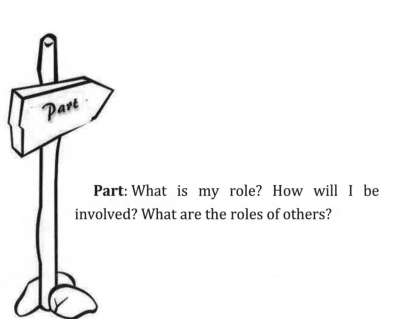

Plan: What is the detailed road map for getting to where we need to go? What is going to happen over the next few months? What happens first, second, third?

Part: What is my role? How will I be involved? What are the roles of others?

PURPOSE

The recruitment process for the team should have included a statement of general purpose. The initial team building process needs to include a discussion of the question, *Why do we exist?* Even with this initial groundwork, though, it is wise to allow the team to engage in a process of clarifying or refining their own purpose statement (often referred to as a mission) before proceeding with the rest of the planning process.

Given the data gathered, both quantitative and qualitative, the specific details of a team's purpose (or mission) may need to be revised. One approach is to present the team with the draft purpose statement and engage the group in giving feedback to ultimately add, delete, and refine the statement until a point of consensus for moving forward with the stated purpose (mission).

CREATING A PICTURE

As has already been shared, a vision is a mental picture of a preferred future. That preferred future must be based on anticipatory vision, not solely on what is past or present. One of the most helpful ways to engage a team in visioning is to have individuals commit five to seven minutes to reflecting on and responding on a pictured future that takes into consideration what one can imagine sensing.

Consider a simple journal prompt as follows:

> *In the year (choose date at least five years in the future), in relation to ministries to, with, and by the sixty-five and older congregation, and preparation of Boomers for this next phase,*

I See...
I Feel...
I Hear...

After individuals have completed writing their vision statements, invite each to read the vision to other team members, with encouragement that other team members listen for themes in what emerges from all. After reading the visions, identify common themes.

An alternative approach to the visioning process is to have each person write his or her vision statement on a sheet of paper silently for several minutes. Each person then passes his or her paper on to a neighbor. The neighbor underlines the key words and phrases they like best. Pass the statements on to the next person, who will also underline key words and phrases. Repeat until everyone has seen (and underlined) everyone else's vision statement. Use a clarifying and combining exercise to get the common phrases and words identified and begin crafting a single vision statement together.

To translate the common themes of a vision statement to the team's desired outcomes, engage team members in writing specific, measurable, and observable desired outcomes, or goals related to each theme.

DEVELOPING A PLAN

The next step for the leadership team is generating possibilities, in order to enable the process of moving toward the desired outcomes. As with finalizing a purpose and vision, there are multiple ways to generate possibilities.

After generating a listing of possibilities, have the group engage in a prioritizing exercise to discern which idea(s) to explore first. This exercise is completed with the gentle reminder that we can do anything, but we can't do everything. A variety of approaches to generating possibilities and prioritizing are provided in Appendix B. Once the top three to five priority action items have been identified, the team can proceed toward developing specific action plans noting what will happen by when and who is responsible.

At this point, it may become necessary to divide a team into subgroups with specific assignments for detailing the plans. It is normal and natural for some to have greater interest and expertise in specific areas.

IMPLEMENTING THE PLAN

A strategy for implementation is often the missing element of a planning process. The excitement that is generated during the visioning exercise and exploring possibilities can wane during the detailing of an action plan. Yet, without implementation, the vision can't happen.

- *Starting up a new initiative amid rapid change has challenges; "Go slow to go fast," is a wise mantra used by many*
- *Start small with your ministry and let the word spread; identify one initiative to pilot. This singular*

effort will help to give focus to content, audience, and needed buy-in from legitimizers (persons whose endorsement can make a difference in the big picture)

- *Engage in an ongoing review and thorough evaluation at its completion to discern needed adjustments or, if necessary, stops*
- *Successes provide stories to validate the new initiative and enable the circle of legitimizers to increase; success stories become the rich soil in which other new initiatives can be planted*
- *Learnings from failure can also be significant. Failures should serve as a shared learning that can be the catalyst for revision of plans and the most effective future launches*

We live in a rapidly changing environment which requires ongoing revision and adaptation of our plans made today. As Jason Silva, a young television personality and filmmaker stated, "There's always going to be the circumstances you can't plan for. There's always the unexpected relevance and the serendipity." For those of us leading in the Christian community, serendipities are acknowledged as gifts from God.

QUESTIONS FOR REFLECTION

Think for yourself...

> What are the assets you could bring to a leadership team for this ministry?

Consider the bigger picture...

> Who are the persons that you believe are ready to assist with launching a new or revamped ministry with older adults? Preparing Boomers for this next phase of life?

Imagine how it could change...

> What challenges might come your way and how might you meet them?

CHAPTER 7

Ideas for a SPICES Ministry

We don't drift in good directions. We discipline and prioritize ourselves there.

~Andy Stanley

*T*here are multiple possibilities for engagement of older adults to live into their purposes all the days of their lives. You can't do everything, so focus becomes important in determining how to best use a team's resources of time and energy. Ask yourselves which of the areas of SPICES needs strengthening?

> ULTIMATELY, THE IDEAL GOAL FOR A SPICES MINISTRY IS TO OFFER EXPERIENCES IN EACH OF THE AREAS....

Ultimately, the ideal goal for a SPICES ministry is to offer experiences in each of the areas: spiritual, physical, intellectual, community, emotional, and service, while maintaining an overall balance.

SPIRITUAL

Implement BLESS, an intentional evangelism approach inspired by Dave Ferguson, author of *"Discover Your Mission Now"*, and used by a number of churches today. Five missional practices make up the acronym BLESS:

- B - Begin with prayer
- L – Listen with care
- E – Eat together
- S – Serve others
- S – Share your story

The BLESS approach to evangelism can be normal, natural relational processes. Encourage Boomers and older adults to create experiences that reach out and BLESS their peers who have not embraced the message of hope in God's Word.

For those who are committed disciples, encourage the pursuit of lifelong growth as a missional disciple through a variety of experiences. Organized Bible studies are important, but also consider the study of church history, worship, and theology. Offer opportunities to stimulate growth in spiritual practices such as prayer, mediation, and journaling.

Small short-term discipleship circles can focus on specific topics.

A mentoring relationship (both as a mentor and a mentee) can stimulate spiritual growth.

A spiritual director may be the most effective means for some.

A creative idea for more access to these experiences in one church is the use of the conference call. Participants with the presenter, engage in the dialogue, and share in prayer, often led by the pastor.

PHYSICAL

A parish nurse ministry can provide a model for the church's engagement with physical wellness. This specialized practice in nursing focuses on the intentional care of the spirit as part of the process of promoting holistic health and preventing or minimizing illness within the congregation.

Included among services for Boomers and older adults could be:

- Health education and teaching
- Fall prevention sessions
- Personal health counseling
- Coordinating events with community health resources
- Organizing health support groups (i.e. cardiac patients, cancer survivors, etc.)
- Response to substance abuse and addictions

Unused space in the church could be used to provide basic exercise equipment. Exercising together can stimulate physical well-being and encourage conversations and building of relationships. Again relating to BLESS, the intentional evangelism strategy mentioned earlier, it could be **exercise together** rather than **eat together**!

A majority of the emerging "new old" today voice a desire to "age in place." Is there an architect in the church or a builder that could provide counsel for people to identify potential need areas for remodeling, in order to have greater accessibility within their current homes?

How can your church partner with the local faith-based retirement communities to access their specialized services such as home care and health education? What faith-based financial planning services are available for consultation with pre-retirees and retirees? The church can and needs to be a connector in this area.

INTELLECTUAL

When creating experiences to stimulate the mind, we must take into consideration visual and hearing issues. Often our sense that older adults aren't interested in learning relates to observing what appears to be disinterest. That disinterest may actually be an inability to hear well or see visuals. Engage in open dialogue with the persons involved and made adjustments in learning approaches as needed.

Some of the possible activities that your church could sponsor to stimulate intellectual growth include:

- Book clubs
- Watching documentaries with follow-up discussion
- Watching films such as CREED and The Intern with discussion about what it says to aging,
- Educational trips
- Discussion groups on topics such as faith and politics or faith and the news
- A "Teach Your Grandparents Day" with younger generations providing tech training and/or tech updates (and older generations teaching their grandchildren culturally forgotten trades and skills)

These offerings can be a great outreach to the community and relate to the "serve others" dimension of the BLESS intentional evangelism strategy.

COMMUNITY

Building community requires more than pot lucks, game nights, and bus trips! Those experiences have a place, but should not be the steady diet. We to need to stimulate community building through exploring topics that provide guidance in establishing new communities.

Guidance could be provided on topics including:

- Recreating community when family and friends die before you
- Reestablishing community when you relocate
- Cultivating NEW relationships without fear
- Developing cross-cultural relationships including special attention to gaining cross-cultural competencies
- Developing intergenerational relationships

Short-term communities can be offered with a focus on topics of common interest such as housing decisions, medical decisions, being a caregiver, grandparenting, financial issues, etc. The experience of "going deeper" with a few can be the pathway to experiencing community in a new way.

EMOTIONAL

The question for those of us working with Boomers and older adults is, "How can we nurture a healthy frame of mind through multiple transitions to avoid isolationism and worthlessness?"

Stephen ministries, spiritual direction, and lay counseling are ongoing ministries for addressing some of the need, but other "just in time" options should be considered.

Some common interests that could form small short-term groups include:

- Exploring identity and purpose
- Managing transitions
    - Empty nesters
    - Grandparenting
    - Adapting to new physical realities
    - Growing a marriage
    - Embracing singleness (or single again)
    - Grief (death or through Alzheimer's or dementia)
    - Caregiving for aging parents or relatives

SERVICE

Engage in dialogue with older adults and you'll find that meaningful service in this phase of life is about more than stuffing envelopes, working in the kitchen, or doing maintenance work at the church. These are viable options, but are not the only ones!

Experiences are needed to help Boomers and older adults discern where their passions and giftedness meet with the need - locally, regionally, and globally. As you plan options for service with older adults, consider both internal and external opportunities.

- Ministries within the church and its local sphere of care -
  - Short-term commitments such as special projects that tap their giftedness, knowledge, and experience
  - Classes and seminars focused on learning to mentor and coach, as well as subsequent pairing with those desiring such a service
  - Classes and seminars to retool or develop new skills for volunteer opportunities
  - Formation of a network of intercessors
  - Care calling (regular phone or in-person visitation with constituents who have mobility issues)
- Ministries beyond -
  - Tutoring and/or mentoring children and youth
  - Regional or global mission trips
  - Educational options to broaden understanding of justice issues such as poverty and mass incarceration
  - Engagement in prison ministries and "pipeline to prison" preventative measures
  - Connection with local agencies engaged in advocacy for seniors – housing, home care services, medical services, legal assistance

ASSISTING THE YOUNGER AND MIDDLE BOOMERS

Although a number of the starter ideas listed for a SPICES framework could be adapted to fit a younger and middle Boomer age group, several key areas need to be added. Some of these additions include:

- Raising awareness about the need for future planning[1] in areas such as;
    - Having conversations about wishes if incapacitated or upon death with parents, children, or trusted friends
    - Financial planning
    - Adapting housing to age in place
- Addressing the myths that create barriers in the growing old process
- Exploring the formation of a new identity and discerning purpose

There is a future to be created. As John F. Kennedy said, "change is the law of life. And those who look only to the past or present are certain to miss the future."

The law of change is real not only for individuals, but also for churches and other organizations.

---

1 Appendices C, D, and E provide further information about these topics

QUESTIONS FOR REFLECTION

Think for yourself . . .

Which 2-3 ideas listed would create a meaningful connection for you in each area of SPICES at this point in your journey?

Consider the bigger picture...

Which dimension(s) of SPICES do you sense need to be enhanced first in your ministry with the sixty-five and older population? And for the trailing edge and middle Boomers?

Imagine how it could change...

If you did not have any existing ministries for the sixty-five and older population, or middle age, how would you start to create a wholistic approach using the SPICES framework?

PART III
EXISTING AND EMERGING
MINISTRIES

Don't be a prisoner of the past, become a pioneer of the future.

~Farshad Asl

CHAPTER 8

Existing Ministries

Real fellowship is more than attending services or having a potluck together. It is experiencing life together.

~PLUS@PCC

*T*he stories that follow are based on the information provided by the founding leaders and/or current leaders of strong, existing ministries for older adults.

PLUS@PCC[1]
A Ministry of Peninsula Covenant Church
Redwood City, California

In early spring 2004, the senior pastor, Gary Gaddini, of Peninsula Covenant Church approached Rod Toews, a staff person at the church, with the request, "Would you begin an older adult ministry?" At the time, more than fifty percent of the congregation of almost 1000 worship attendees was over fifty years of age.

The first step was to contact an outside consultant, Alan Forsman. Twenty adults, age fifty and over, were invited to

---

[1] *Information provided by Rod Toews, founding leader of PLUS*

gather and talk about a potential ministry. The consultant attended the next organizational meeting and a subsequent meeting with twelve selected potential leaders to formulate a plan.

The name, PLUS, was chosen with a mission articulated as follows:

> "A community of those over fifty in which God's purposes for their lives are fulfilled through fellowship, spiritual growth, service and fun."

September 2004 was set as the PLUS launch date.

From the church directory, a potential list of participants was selected and they were invited to a free launch luncheon of PLUS with the explanation of "we want to add a PLUS to their lives."

The potential ministry was outlined and the leaders were introduced. Overall, people were enthusiastic and affirmed the ministry.

During the course of ten years after its beginnings, PLUS was developed to address the felt needs of the persons involved. Activities included Sunday school classes by age, concerts, fellowship, and fun activities, discipleship, outreach, mission trips, and international tours. One of the key desired outcomes was achieved – people in the fifty plus age group were made to feel significant! The ministry is now being led by a new pastor. New vision with new ideas has shaped new programming.

PEOPLE IN THE FIFTY PLUS AGE GROUP WERE MADE TO FEEL SIGNIFICANT!

Yet, the mission remains the same.

PLUS@PCC continues to be a community of those over fifty in which God's purposes for their lives are fulfilled through fellowship, spiritual growth, service, and fun.

TREK[1]
Harbor Covenant Church
Gig Harbor, Washington

The seeds for TREK, a ministry for those fifty plus, were planted at a staff retreat when the group identified and discussed a growing nationwide population emerging with 10,000 people turning sixty-five years of age each day in our country. Considering this fact and the significant number of older adults already attending Harbor Covenant Church, the Senior Pastor, Michael White and Sammi McCubbins, the Director of Pastoral Care, began to discuss the need for an older adult ministry that would connect older adults attending Harbor Covenant and reach out to older adults in the community.

Sammi began to pray about whom to ask to serve on such a team and how such a ministry would incorporate the church's organizing principles: *reach people for Christ, make disciples and live a lifestyle of compassion, mercy, and justice.*

First, older adults who were thinking about retiring or who had recently retired were invited to a *Success to Significance* luncheon that focused on how older adults today were moving beyond the first half, in the game of life, into a time of revitalization. People who attended this luncheon and who were interested in this more vibrant older adult lifestyle were invited to join this upcoming older adult ministry leadership team along with other hand-picked team members.

The leadership team met for eighteen months before the launching of the older adult ministry named TREK with a

---

[1] *Information provided by Sammi McCubbins, Director of Pastoral Care*

purpose of being a group of people who enjoy being together having fun while growing in their faith and reaching out to people in the community. It was launched during fall kick-off with a special celebration and a calendar of events that invited people to join in the TREK activities. Dimensions that have emerged include:

- Building fellowship among people both inside and outside the church which encourages inviting friends and neighbors to the TREK excursions
- Providing relevant enrichment opportunities appropriate for older adult living through forums, speakers and classes (spiritual, financial, family)
- Creating recreational outings that attract older adults and build community
- Involving older adults in service projects in the community

The signs of effectiveness with TREK have included:

- The growing level of enthusiasm expressed by the leadership team since launching the ministry
- Growing efforts to invite friends from outside the church to TREK events
- "Let's do this again" (positive feedback from attendees)
- "We need more tables" (higher than expected turnout to events)

The future hope for TREK is continued effectiveness in current dimensions with expansion into service, outreach, and collaborative efforts.

The name, TREK, signals moving forward and that is the nature of the individuals participating, as well as the team providing leadership. As the church's website description of TREK ends:

Life is an adventure ... Join us!

Drop in Day
Evangelical Covenant Church
Springfield, Massachusetts[1]

Drop in Day is an eagerly anticipated weekly experience. Every Thursday fifty to sixty older adults come to the church for a comprehensive day of study, exercise, healthy nutrition, and a sense of community.

Over seventeen years ago, two laypersons, then in their late sixties and early seventies, approached Brian, another layperson, whose team was providing a meal for Wednesday night activities with a question that launched the ministry.

Would he consider doing something on a Thursday noon for an emerging older adult population?

The affirmative response led to what is now a growing, balanced ministry.

People start arriving at 9:00 A.M. and engage in conversation over coffee. Bible Study begins at 9:30 A.M. For many attendees, this is their weekly worship experience, as they come from the surrounding neighborhoods and don't otherwise attend church.

The ministry was originally called Triple Zip, since there was intention from the beginning to focus on three zip codes around the church. The demographics of the surrounding area now afford a wonderful opportunity for an increasingly multi-cultural, multi-generational experience.

A wholistic approach has emerged. In addition to the Bible study there are table games, additional devotions and prayer, Tai Chi and other fitness opportunities, freshly prepared lunches, and deepening relationships.

---

[1] *Information provided by Brian Wilkens, lay leader*

The current leadership team is multi-generational with laypersons from their fifties to eighties. The pastor experiences strong support. Words that describe Drop in Day include:

- Identity
- Purpose
- Health
- Spiritual Growth
- Fun
- Community

. . . and gratitude.

CHAPTER 9

Emerging Ministries

There needed to be something that met the spiritual needs of older adults, not just in the church, but for the local community as well.

~Renee Roeschley

*T*he stories that follow are based on information provided by the current leaders of emerging ministries in the area of older adult ministry.

JOURNEYS For Adults 50+[1]
Salem Covenant Church
New Brighton, Minnesota

The seeds for JOURNEYS were planted during the church's strategic planning process initiated by the Leadership Team to discern what areas of focus would help their church increase effectiveness in fulfilling its mission. The result from a look at the external community was that one of the largest and fastest growing populations in the church's community was people headed into retirement. This also was one of the largest percentages within the existing congregation.

---

[1] *Information provided by Jonna Fantz, staff, and Sue Poston, team leader for JOURNEYS*

Internally, the current Senior Fellowship Team, while implementing great monthly Friday lunch events, were noticing declining numbers and an increasing average age of the older adults that attended. The Senior Fellowship ministry team stated they knew that something needed to be done for older adults who didn't have mobility issues, but that was just not what their team was called to do.

At the end of the strategic planning process, the outreach and community life pastor, Jonna Fantz was charged with "getting the ball rolling" to form a new ministry team. After conversations with Jonna and the senior pastor, Mark Pattie, Sue Poston, an active retiree engaged in a vital life of her own, committed to serve as leader of this new team.

Sue was motivated by the challenge to chart a new way to do ministry to people in the third phase of their adult lives. Sue also felt like she had not connected well with her own peer group in this age. She sensed this was an invitation from God to connect more deeply, herself, while helping others to do the same.

Forming a Leadership Team specifically for this new ministry was a priority. Sue and Jonna brainstormed a listing of potential team members. They added to that list other people whose voices needed to be heard. An invitation was sent for a focus group and dessert night. Twelve people attended that session.

Sue guided the conversation and Jonna recorded on newsprint ideas that surrounded four questions:

- What is it that you are currently involved in that brings meaning and joy to your life?

- What are you hungry to know more about?
- What issues are you confronting?
- What is missing for your age group in Salem's ministries in these three areas:
  - o SPIRITUAL FORMATION
  - o FUN AND FELLOWSHIP
  - o SERVICE
- Share general comments, hopes, dreams, fears, etc.

The evening stimulated great conversation with honest and open sharing. Sue followed up by pursuing people who attended that evening to be on the team, and others that couldn't attend the focus group, but were interested. A team of ten persons joined Sue for the adventure of building this new ministry.

Salem Covenant then extended an invitation to Evelyn Johnson and Alan Forsman to lead a retreat to launch this new leadership team. They were to provide some education to help this team learn more about this demographic and to inspire them toward a vision of what was possible in this ministry. They also were tasked with helping the team to build community and begin the ministry planning process.

The team met on a Saturday in late February for six hours. It was a powerful time of launching and bonding. There was lots of great learning and key issues emerged, such as how to name the ministry. The team engaged in great discussion about the older adult demographic and what aging myths existed in Salem Covenant Church. The team agreed to meet again following Easter.

The first regular team meeting ended up focusing on what kind of event should be done as an interest raising event.

JOURNEYS For Adults 50+ emerged as the name of the ministry with a stated purpose:

> *JOURNEYS exists to provide connecting opportunities through a wholistic ministry within and beyond the Salem community to strengthen spiritual growth, stimulate intellectual curiosity, promote healthy living, and enrich social, community and missional involvement.*

As meetings progressed, the team decided to do a survey on Sunday morning and offer cinnamon rolls as a hospitality and gathering piece.

To date, the key outcome from JOURNEYS For Adults 50+ has been a team which has bonded and is full of good ideas.

The future is embedded in the phrase, *"coming soon."*

With Age...[1]
A Collaborative Ministry
Chicago, Illinois

Senior Share, a formation group for older adults at Grace Covenant Church in Chicago, was started in 2003 by Renee Roeschley. In the beginning, the make-up of the group was primarily people from the church. However, as the years passed, its composition evolved and now most members of the group are from the local community. During the process of leading this group, Renee noted the importance of older adults having a place to meet spiritual needs through sharing and reflecting on God's presence in their life stories with peers.

She also began to notice that there were a limited number of ministries available, and even those that had started in the local church for older adults were not sustained. Another observation was the absence of a "place" for older adults at many levels in the church, much like what it looks like in our society.

Renee became burdened with a sense that there could be so much more than what is offered for older adults, in the church, by the government agencies, and through nonprofits. There needed to be something that met the spiritual needs of older adults, not just in the church, but for the local community as well. She believed the church was the perfect vessel to do this.

Renee always felt that she could not start something like this alone. No one "caught the vision," until she shared it with

---

[1] *Information provided by Renee Roeschley and Mary Jane Dawson, Leaders*

Mary Jane Dawson who co-facilitates the Senior Share group at Grace.

They did not follow up on this desire until summer of 2015, when—in a coaching session with Troy Cady of the nonprofit, "Playfull"—Renee talked about it. Troy sensed her passion and the vision that God had entrusted to her. Troy encouraged her to think of others that could join her in collaborating. She invited Mary Jane for more conversation and, together, they began to plan a time when others would be invited to a series of listening groups to discuss the needs of older adults.

During coaching sessions with Troy, Renee and Mary Jane made a list of people to invite to be part of a group to explore the needs of older adults in Chicago. Many accepted their invitation and the first meeting was in October of 2015.

In the group there are and have been social workers, pastors, people who work directly with older adults in a facility environment, and several older adults of various backgrounds such as teaching, administration and banking.

In the time since Troy finished coaching the two women and leading the listening group exploration, Renee and Mary Jane have taken turns leading parts of each meeting and are inviting other members who are willing to lead certain topics.

One of the first steps was discerning a mission statement for the group with all team members contributing in the creating of a draft, revising, and ultimately affirming a final mission. At the same time, the group generated a listing of potential names for the ministry and—by consensus—affirmed the chosen name.

Thus, the birth of the new collaborative ministry with a name and a mission:

WITH AGE...

> *"Our mission is to create a space where older adults explore and affirm their identity and purpose, find voice and grow spiritually as engaged members of their communities."*

During the process, some of the noteworthy dimensions of ministry that are emerging include:

- Serving populations: newly retired and older
- Programs or ministries started by *With Age...*, and potentially with the church, for the local community on the north side of Chicago
- Projects that focus on exploring purpose and identity at "this time in life"

In a reasonable projected amount of time, the group plans to use one or two of the proposed programs that were identified in the process of the listening groups facilitated by Troy Cady. At the present time, Renee and Mary Jane are assessing the strengths of the core group to determine what skills and strengths exist in setting up the programs, advertising them, and other details necessary to carry them out.

Before the programs are started, attendance goals will be set. In addition, evaluations will be requested from those who attend to adequately monitor, 1) staying true to the mission of *With Age...*, and 2) to aid the implementation team in making needed changes and to determine if the programs are making a difference.

To date, the key outcomes have been:

- a solid and dedicated core group of six to seven individuals that work well together
- a name, mission statement, and twice monthly meetings
- several proposed programs that align with the mission statement

In summary, creating *With Age...* has been a process of observing older adults, discerning personal passions, receiving coaching, listening to the voices of others, sharing ideas, and deciding together!

All of these steps have shaped the hope to fully develop programming by the end of 2016 for implementation in early 2017.

AN INSIDE LOOK AT AGING [1]
For Middle Adults
A Plan for Helping with the Task of Caregiving

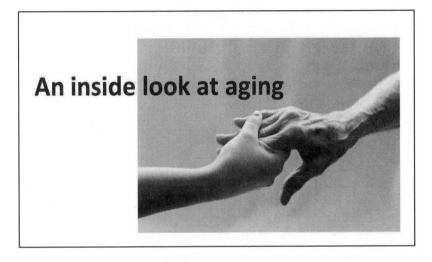

We live in a youth-obsessed culture. But what does life look like for those who are in the later phase of aging? This is a key question if we are to engage with, serve and learn from those who are older adults.

For those of us with aging parents, as well as those of us who are looking ahead to the later seasons of life, getting some perspective on aging can be a source of help, comfort and motivation.

The two one-hour sessions were designed to focus on the challenges and opportunities of aging in today's society and solutions and perspectives.

The first session explored a wide range of topics including:

---

[1] *Information was provided by Steve Wong, designer and teacher of the sessions.*

- Thinking about aging using a TED talk, *"What really matters at the end of life"*
- Describing aging using the author Atul Gawande's book, *"Being Mortal"*, Erik Erikson's eight stages, and reflections on 1 John 2:12-14
- A case study in aging focused on Felix Silverstone, from Atul Gawande's book
- The local church and those who are aging with reflections on the SPIES framework given in this book

The second session focused on external solutions and internal perspectives. Resources used included:

- *"Brief but Spectacular"* video by Flossie Lewis[1]
- Dr. Bill Thomas's story
- General information about assisted living from *"Being Mortal"*
- Excerpts from Joan Chittister's book, *"The Gift of Years"*
- Joan Erikson's summary of a ninth stage addition, gerotranscendence, to her husband, Erik's, original eight stages.

---

[1] *Flossie Lewis' story is one of the "Brief but Spectacular" series of videos shown on the "PBS Newshour" at http://www.pbs.org/newshour/brief/page/3 or on YouTube: https://www.youtube.com/watch?v=oeUc7hjYLbl.*

At the close of the second session, the question to be asked is "What are up to three things that I will do in the next couple of weeks as a result of these sessions and why?"

Since the initial preparation of the sessions, Pastor Wong has expanded the series to three sessions with addition of more information regarding the ninth stage.

~~~~

There is much on the horizon to celebrate, anticipate, and create. *Let's wake up, join these pioneers, and go confidently into the future!*

PART IV
RESOURCES AND REFLECTING

"To God be the glory, great things He hath done."

~ Hymn by Frances Jane "Fanny" Crosby

LIST OF APPENDICES

APPENDIX A

Older Adult Ministry Team

Purpose: to gain input that will assist congregational leadership in discerning God's spiritual, strategic direction for the future of ministry by, with and for older adults

People: usually comprised of 5-9, or 3-5 in a smaller church. The team is appointed (preferred). One member from leadership team or staff should be present as a liaison. The Older Adult Ministry Team is appointed by the church leadership team (LT) and is a recommending body whose findings will serve as input to the LT in their discernment of future direction.

Process: the team engages in assessing the internal environment of the congregation and external environments represented by the unique regions of the members and attendees. The focus is on determining the appropriate demographics.

Attention is given to learning from our history in order to inform our future. Throughout the process, "transparent" communication is essential. An intentional prayer effort should undergird all the work. The benefits are many. Fresh information is gathered. Current assumptions are verified or contradicted. Action indicates that there is a future and "we are moving ahead."

General tasks of the process are:

- Gathering fresh information--taking a new look at the current reality
- Maintenance--evaluating current ministries
- Enhancement --focus on a significant area (areas) which can engender future hope
- Readiness-- assessing history, identity, leadership, outside resources, new direction, openness to change

Related tasks include:

- Reducing Anxiety
- Assessing Infrastructures
- Attending to matters of Whole-Life Stewardship (which includes spiritual growth, service and giving)
- Enhancing Leadership Skills
- Focusing on Spiritual Needs (Prayer, Discipleship, Healing)

Participants:

- Positive influencers
- Intergenerational representation-from 50s-70s is recommended
- Diversity in gender, ethnicity, and time in the church (fresh eyes and ears encouraged)

Process:

- An initial orientation session to communicate the process and begin the work
- A monthly meeting to receive updates on progress
- Engaging a wider range of people in gathering information
- Working in subgroups according to interest and expertise
- Collating information and begin interpretation of the results-what patterns are emerging
- Send findings and recommendations to the LT
- Get buy in from LT and implement

APPENDIX B

Brainstorming and Prioritizing

Brainstorming

Nonjudgmental brainstorming is an effective way to gain input from a team. There are several effective processes.

ROUND ROBIN APPROACH

- The round robin approach works best with up to fifteen people. For more than that, additional groups could be created.
- Frame the question (i.e. "What type of activity would interest you?" or "What type of experience would meet your felt needs?")
- Craft a question for each of the areas in SPICES.
- Give people a couple of minutes to think. Ask for a volunteer to start. Stress that only one idea is shared initially. After the first person volunteers, set a pattern and go around the group until all ideas are stated.

Someone should facilitate the process and another should record the ideas on a flip chart or white board. Guidelines for brainstorming should be:

1. All ideas are honored and recorded
2. No debating of ideas as they are stated

After all ideas are recorded, there can be a process of clarifying and combining in preparation for a focusing activity.

AFFINITY DIAGRAM

Affinity diagrams are an alternative method of brainstorming.

- Frame the question as for brainstorming.
- Each person is given two large post-it notes. After having a couple of minutes to think, they are to write one idea on each post-it. Ideas should be brief and should start with an actionable verb, i.e. improve communication, conduct focus groups, know our neighborhood.
- Collect the post-it notes, searching for group similarities and themes.
- Create categories from the clustered post-it notes.
- Discuss ideas for clarification.

FOCUSING

Whatever information gathering processes are used, it is essential to prioritize. A proven method to narrow an idea is "Divide by 3."

- Tabulate the total number of consolidated ideas. Divide by 3. If there are twenty-four ideas the number would be eight. Each person gets eight dots. There is one dot per vote. Walk around and place dots on the ideas (on post-its or flip charts). All dots should go on different ideas.
- There tends to be a cluster of three to five top ideas. From there, a next step would be a simple rank order. People can vote again, either with dots or with raising of hands to determine a consensus on top ideas.
- The votes should result in three areas for exploration.

APPENDIX C

End of Life Decisions and Having Conversations

"Later..."
"When the need arises..."
"All's well..."
"Not yet..."
"I'm too busy living..."

One or more of these responses may be what you've heard a spouse, parent, child, or friend say. Perhaps even you have said it. Unfortunately, those comments, and others like them, are common for a large segment of our population, when it comes to the area of communicating with family members and trusted friends about one's wishes, should he or she become incapacitated or die. In a recent Harris Survey completed for the National Endowment of Financial Services in March 2016, only 33% of the population of all ages have engaged in a conversation about this inevitable stage of life. The time is NOW, not later.

One of the first considerations for such a conversation is determining a Power of Attorney (POA). POA should be secured with legal advice, as opposed to simply completing a form found online. Different states have varying standards for types of Powers of Attorney and what they are allowed or not allowed to do.

Besides POAs for financial and legal matters, one should identify a medical or health care power of attorney. Medical or health care POAs are those trusted people named to make decisions for you when you are unable to do so.

Regardless of the type of POA, the missing link is often communication between spouses, parent and child, or trusted friends. Communication is needed for clarity and release from anxiety on the part of both.

In addition, one needs to maintain a clear, comprehensive list of assets, liabilities, account numbers, online account sign-in information (including usernames, passwords, and associated emails), insurance policies, and location of wills and trusts. Review the list with the chosen responsible person(s) who will be faced with a multitude of financial transactions and decisions upon your being incapacitated or dying.

Lastly, writing out your wishes for burial and discussing those wishes with one's spouse, children, or a trusted representative is another critical task on the "to do list." This becomes an extension of your care for them beyond your death. The immediate hours after one's death are filled with an overwhelming checklist for those responsible for burial. Providing this overview can alleviate anxiety and allow close family and friends to engage in the necessary work of mourning.

Having a conversation about being incapacitated or one's post-death wishes will be much easier to have if it is not an imminent possibility. However, if you are already in poor health, it is not too late to have the conversation.

APPENDIX D

Assessing Finances and Preparing A Plan

We sing "Praise God from whom all blessings flow," and yet we often lose touch with the reality that all blessings in life are a gift from God including our wealth. Whether our wealth is large or small, we have a responsibility to be good stewards throughout life. As we enter the later phase of life we may wonder, *Do I have enough? Will I outlive my funds? Am I prepared for the unexpected?*

These are not easy questions to answer. They take faith and wise counsel, not just from a financial planner, but from other Christians who can give input as to how faith and love of God can find expression in the way we manage our finances. Underlying all of our planning are the key questions:

- *Does our use of wealth increase the capacity for others to be blessed?*
- *Have I provided for the continued blessing of others after my death?*

Although it is desirable to be engaged in financial planning during all of one's adult life, it is especially important to give this area attention during the middle age years. Some of the key steps to take include:

1. Take an inventory of your financial resources
2. Design a retirement income strategy
3. Prepare a projected budget for later years
4. Anticipate the unexpected
5. Review your will and/or trust (and if you don't have a will, NOW is the time)

There are many tools available today through secular financial institutions to help with the details of financial planning, but it is the Christian community—found in churches and other Christian organizations including Christian financial services—that can provide the needed input for making choices that will be God-honoring. Early planning allows one to continue living as a good steward of God's resources all the days of one's life and beyond.

Adapting Housing for Accessibility

Aging in place is increasingly becoming the desired approach among the sixty-five and older population. People want to stay in the communities where they have built relationships and often in the homes where they made their life's memories.

For many, moving to an "accessible" home may not be a feasible option from a financial perspective or desire to retain social connections, so thinking through adaptations that could be made in an existing home may be the best first step.

We go to the doctor for regular check-ups. Why not pursue a "residence accessibility" check-up? A simple accessibility checklist might include discerning ways to create:

- ✓ Use of stairs for access to other levels
- ✓ Open walkways and hallways
- ✓ Wide doorways
- ✓ Pathways for ramps to outside
- ✓ Safety in the bathroom
- ✓ Ease in use of kitchen and laundry

If one is seeking to buy or rent a residence in a new location, a "what to look for" checklist will help narrow the potentials. The "accessibility" checklist noted above can be used for assessing the residence, but one needs to also determine if the location provides:

- ✓ Safety and security
- ✓ Sense of community
- ✓ Affordable economy
- ✓ Available work and volunteer opportunities
- ✓ Public transportation
- ✓ Accessible healthcare services

The design and location of a residence can negatively impact one's health and well-being if it hinders fulfilling daily tasks and/or limits socialization. The old adage applies to preparing for accessible living: *Don't put off until tomorrow what can be done today.*

REFERENCES

2016 *Alzheimer's Disease Facts and Figures.* Alzheimer's Association.

AARP *Public Policy Institute and National Conference of State Legislatures Research Report,* 2011.

"Ageism." *Dictionary.com.* Random House Unabridged Dictionary, 2015. Web. May. 2016.

Andrew J. Martin, Harry Nejad, Susan Colmar and Gregory Arief D. Liem (2012). *Adaptability: Conceptual and Empirical Perspectives on Responses to Change, Novelty and Uncertainty.* Australian Journal of Guidance and Counselling, 22, pp 58-81. doi:10.1017/jgc.2012.8.

"Andy Stanley." *BrainyQuote.* Xplore. Web. 2016.

Barna, George and Kinnaman, David. *"Churchless: Understanding Today's Unchurched and How to Connect with Them."* October 1 2014. Print.

Boice, James Montgomery. *Daniel: An Expositional Commentary.* 2003. Print.

Brenner, Joanna, and Aaron Smith. *"72% of Online Adults Are Social Networking Site Users."* Pew Research Center Internet Science Tech RSS. Pew Research Center, 05 Aug. 2013. Web. 6 June 2016

Bridges, William. *Managing Transitions: Making Sense of Life's Changes.* 2004. DeCapo Press, division of Peresus Books. Cambridge, MA

Calhoun, Adele Ahlberg. *Spiritual Disciplines Handbook: Practices That Transform Us.* IVP Books, an Imprint of InterVarsity Press, 2015.

"Canadian Longitudinal Study on Aging." Web. June 2016.

Chittister, Joan. *The Gift of Years: Growing Older Gracefully.* New York, NY: BlueBridge, 2008. Print.

Crosby, Franny. "To God Be the Glory." *Hymnary.org.* The Hymn Society, 2007. Web. 2016.

Cumming, Elaine, and William E. Henry. *Growing Old.* New York: Arno, 1961. Print.

"Dave Workman." *BrainyQuote.* Xplore. Web. 2016.

De Pree, Max. *Leadership Is an Art.* East Lansing, MI: Michigan State U, 1987. Print.

Dweck, Carol S. *Mindset: The New Psychology of Success.* New York: Random House, 2006. Print.

Erikson, Erik H. *Childhood and Society.* New York: Norton, 1964. Print.

Erikson, Erik H. and Erikson, Joan. *The Life Cycle Completed (Extended Version).* New York: Norton, 1998. Print.

"Farshad Asl." *BrainyQuote*. Xplore. Web. 2016.

Foster, Richard J. *Celebration of Discipline*. London: Hodder & Stoughton, 1980. Print.

Gladwell, Malcolm. *Outliers: The Story of Success*. New York: Little, Brown, 2008. Print.

Hanson, Amy. *Boomers and Beyond: Tapping the Ministry Talents and Passions of Adults over Fifty*. San Francisco, CA: Jossey-Bass, 2010. Print.

"Jason Silva." *BrainyQuote*. Xplore. Web. 2016.

"John F. Kennedy." *BrainyQuote*. Xplore. Web. 2016.

Larkin, Marilyn "Brain and Behavior Are Modifiable, Even as We Get Older." Elsevier Connect. May 2015. Web. June 2016. Columbia Aging Center at Columbia University.

"NetWellness." NetWellness. University of Ohio, n.d. Web. May 2016.

"Niko Kazantzakis." *BrainyQuote*. Xplore. Web. 9 Oct. 2015.

Nouwen, Henri J. M. *Life of the Beloved: Spiritual Living in a Secular World*. Crossroads Publishing. 1992. New York, NY. Print.

Nouwen, Henri J. M. *Lifesigns: Intimacy, Fecundity, and Ecstasy in Christian Perspective*. Garden City. N.Y.: Doubleday, 1986. Print.

Ortman, Jennifer M., Victoria A. Velkoff, and Howard Hogan. *"An Aging Nation: The Older Population in the United States."* U.S. Census Bureau. U.S. Census Bureau, May 2014. Web. June 2016.

Palmer, Parker J. *Let Your Life Speak: Listening for the Voice of Vocation*. San Francisco: Jossey-Bass, 2000. Print.'

Peck, M. Scott. *The Different Drum: Community-Making and Peace*. Arrow, 1987.

"Ralph Waldo Emerson." *BrainyQuote*. Xplore. Web. Oct. 2015.

"Retirement." *Dictionary.com*. Random House Unabridged Dictionary, 2015. Web. November. 2015.

"Social Security History." *Social Security*. Social Security Administration, 11 Apr. 2012. Web. 2015.

Ten Boom, Corrie, John L. Sherrill, and Elizabeth Sherrill. *The Hiding Place*. Washington Depot, CT: Chosen, 1971. Print.

The English Standard Version Bible. New York: Oxford University Press, 2009. Print.

"The Holy Bible." New International Version. Grand Rapids, MI: Zondervan Corporation, 2010. Web. Oct. 2015.

Tournier, Paul. *Learn to Grow Old*. New York: Harper & Row, 1972. Print.

"Volunteering in 2014 : The Economics Daily." U.S. Bureau of Labor Statistics. U.S. Bureau of Labor Statistics, n.d. Web. June 2016.

Waldinger, Robert. *"What Makes a Good Life? Lessons from the Longest Study on Happiness"* Harvard University. Web. December 2015.

RESOURCES

Books

Being Mortal, 2014 from Henry Holt & Company, By Atul Gawande

Canoeing the Mountains, 2015 from IVP Books, By Tod Bolsinger

Disrupt Aging: A Bold New Path to Living Your Best Life at Every Age, April 2016, by JoAnn Jenkins, CEO of AARP

Falling Upward, A Spirituality for the Two Halves of Life, 2011, by Richard Rohr

Life Reimagined: Discovering Your New Life Possibilities, Sep 6, 2013, by Richard J. Leider and Alan M. Webber

Managing Oneself, 2008 from Harvard Business Review Classics, By Peter Drucker

Shaping a Life of Significance for Retirement, Jan 1, 2010, by Jack Hansen and Jerry P Haas

The Next America, 2015, by Paul Taylor and the PEW Research Center

Third Calling: What are you doing the rest of your life?, August 2016,by Richard and Leona Bergstrom

Third Calling Study Guide, December 2016, by Richard and Leona Bergstrom

What Got You Here, Won't Get You There: How Successful People Become Even More Successful, 2007 from Hachette books, By Marshall Goldsmith

Websites

changingaging.com

encore.org

lifereimagined.aarp.org

milkeninstitute.org/centers/the-center-for-the-future-of-aging

nextavenue.org

re-ignite.net

Other Media

Brief But Spectacular, Creator: Steve Goldbloom. Videographer: Zach Land-Miller. Featuring: Flossie Lewis. PBS Newshour, April 5, 2016.

Purposeful Aging: A Model for a New Life Course, October 2015 Study by the Center for the Future of Aging, Paul Irving, Chair at www.milkeninstitute.org/publications/view/760

What Makes a Good Life? Lessons from the Longest Study on Happiness, YouTube, TED Talk Electronically Published 25 Jan. 2016.

IN REFLECTION

Writing and researching for this book was a wondrous journey. Interacting with people about the philosophy and framework of a wholistic approach was energizing. This led to the development of a seminar entitled Crescendo, capturing the idea of an ascent to a good ending. Ultimately, a one-year pilot project evolved in collaboration with our denomination.

Since the release of *"Regenerating Generations"*, we have worked with our colleague, Debbie Blue, on refining the seminar. A seven-person team of Crescendo coaches joined us as co-leaders of seminars and engaged in follow-up with participating churches The pilot seminar followed the basic outline of the original book, Its purpose was to equip pastors and local church leaders to address:

- The barriers created by ageism in our local churches
- Preparation of 52-64 year olds for effective transitioning to the next phase of adulthood
- Opportunities for meaningful engagement of the 65+ constituency in personal growth as disciples who makes disciples

Over two hundred persons from forty-eight churches attended seven pilot seminars in four major geographic regions. The coaches made follow-up phone contact with local leaders to determine next steps. Over half of the participating churches have indicated a desire for some type of on-site follow-up.

Our hope in writing the original book was to encourage and equip local church leaders to have conversations about engaging older adults in purposeful living all the days of their lives. We have witnessed those conversations first-hand during these seminars.

Our personal observations during this pilot project have both confirmed and expanded our knowledge. Paul Tournier's advice that people should start preparing for this last phase in their forties and fifties is definitely worth heeding. Ministries to assist Boomers with their multiple transitions is a requirement, not an option. The awareness of changing demographics and pervasive myths related to aging needs to be increased. Biblical examples of purposeful living at advanced ages must be explored to understand God's intent for all the days of our lives.

Also, the need for CRESCENDO in our Spanish-speaking churches was validated. Many seminar materials have been translated and several seminars led in Spanish only. The SPIES framework evolved to be SPICES for more emphasis on Community and Service. Older participants experienced "aha moments" in being reminded that God has purpose for their lives in this later phase.

In addition to the input from seminars, we have gained input from focus groups and an introductory webinar led with our colleague, Debbie Blue.

This last year has helped us further define reality. Some of those learnings include:

- Current older adult ministries in our churches are sporadic and primarily focused on social and personal care
- Ministries to assist Boomers with their multiple life transitions are almost nonexistent
- Boomers and older adults (70+) want to engage, but not in traditional ways
- Local churches need resourcing to increase awareness and explore the potential of boomers and older adults to engage in missional discipleship

The end result of the findings through the pilot project is the endorsement of CRESCENDO to become an integral part of the Make and Deepen Disciples mission priority of the Evangelical Covenant Church. The whole of the process has been a crescendo.

This has been a team effort and we want to acknowledge and express our gratitude to many persons – both in terms of this rerelease as well as the original book. Among those related specifically to this rerelease are:

- Debbie Blue, our friend, colleague, and mentor in many areas, whose willingness to share leadership of the pilot with us has been especially meaningful
- At our denominational offices in Chicago:

○ Michelle Sanchez, Executive Minister of Make and Deepen Disciples, whose passion to create a multiethnic movement of disciples of all ages who engage in missional discipleship continues to inspire and encourage us

○ Ed Gilbreath, Executive Director of Communications, to whom we believe God gave the word, crescendo, as the term to embrace what we were seeking to emphasize

From the West Coast, Midwest, and Central regions of the United States, we are grateful to a number of people, including: Lynda Delgado (Los Angeles), Ron Short (Sacramento), Stanley Long (Bay Area), Sharon Stenger (Sacramento), Lynn Black (McPherson, KS), Lisa Caridine (Chicago), and Harold Spooner (Chicago) – the team of seven CRESCENDO coaches who organized and managed pilot events, recruited participants, assumed follow-up responsibilities, and shared in visioning for the future.

Also, from throughout the United States and Canada: Seminar, focus group, and webinar participants who invested time to attend, participate fully, and share evaluations to stimulate our learnings.

In relation to the original manuscript, we continue to acknowledge and express gratitude to:

- Reji Laberje for initiating the idea of putting our thoughts on paper, guiding us with her "know how" and leading the way for this rerelease. And, to her whole team for their support in publication.
- Millie Lungren, Debbie Blue, and Carolyn Pitezel, friends and ministry colleagues, for investing time in reviewing and editing the original manuscript to guide our revisions.
- Contributors to the book—most of whom are from the West Coast and Chicago—where, together, we've had more recent ministries.

Our gratitude for specific contributions includes the following:

Vital Life Stories
Lenore Three Stars – Spokane, Washington
Will Davidson – San Ramon, California
Jim Gaderlund – Los Altos, California
Sharon Stenger – Roseville, California
Jorge Maldonado – Spring Valley, California
Sharon Davis – Jackson, Mississippi (formerly Chicago)
Allan and Joyce Anderson – Santa Barbara, California
Stanley Long – Fremont, California
Paul Larsen – Rancho Mirage, California
Rod Toews – Turlock, California
Marv Gibbs – Hong Kong

Existing and Emerging Ministries
PLUS –*Redwood City, California*
TREK –*Gig Harbor, Washington*
DROP IN DAY – *Springfield, Massachusetts*
JOURNEYS – *New Brighton, Minnesota*
WITH AGE... - *Chicago, Illinois*
AN INSIDE LOOK AT AGING – *Los Altos, California*

To the models of vital living throughout our lives – grandparents, parents, siblings, and close friends/mentors. The process of embracing our own aging and wanting to help others do so began during interactions with these persons.

And, to our supportive spouses (Sara who continues modeling vitality just as her mother Isabelle did and Phil, now among the cloud of witnesses, who modeled vital living in the midst of multiple physical losses). Without the freedom to "fly here and there," these thirty plus years of partnering in ministry might not have been possible. The partnering provided many of the experiences and persons that are reflected in this book and enabled the launching of a pilot project to test the ideas.

The Evangelical Covenant Church, our denominational family, is committed to joining God in His mission to see more disciples, among more populations, in a more caring and just world. We are thankful for our denomination's efforts to address sexism and racism in the process of pursuing that mission. Now is the time for, not only the Evangelical Covenant Church, but all church bodies to address ageism as well. It is not only the vitality of individuals that is at stake, but also the vitality of congregations in advancing Christ's mission.

ABOUT THE AUTHORS

Dr. Alan Forsman

Alan, currently residing in Sarasota, Florida, has over thirty years of experience in organizational consulting. He specializes in executive coaching, as well as team development, facilitation, and training. In addition to his ongoing multifaceted ministry of coaching and facilitating he serves on the leadership team for CRESCENDO, a ministry of Make and Deepen Disciples of the Evangelical Covenant Church focused on mobilizing boomers and older adults as missional disciples.

He has studied gerontology and taught adult ministries including emphasis on older adults at the seminary level. He has both started four older adult ministries while serving churches and consulted with several churches in starting older adult ministries.

Alan is married to Sara and they have lived in seven states. Regeneration for Alan and Sara comes, not just from their active lives of service, but also from more than twenty nieces and nephews who keep them abreast of current trends while providing mutual mentoring and interacting around life skills and technology assistance.

Evelyn M.R. Johnson

Evelyn, currently residing in Chicago, Illinois, is an ordained minister in the Evangelical Covenant Church. She stepped aside in 2015 from traditional compensated employment after serving for forty-two years in local church, regional conference, and denominational roles. Evelyn serves now as a member of the leadership team for CRESCENDO, a ministry of Make and Deepen Disciples of the Evangelical Covenant Church, focused on mobilizing boomers and older adults as missional disciples.

Evelyn is passionate about visioning and translating that vision to action for the purpose of advancing Kingdom-building ministry. Evelyn loves to assist persons in navigating changes with a focus on living joyfully through transitions.

Evelyn was married to Phil for almost fifty-two years at the time of his death in 2014. She has two married sons, two daughters-in-law, and four grandchildren. Email, texting and social media are definitely a part of her vital life!

Debbie C. Blue

After more than twenty-three years in the hospital environment, Debbie entered into full-time ministry and joined a team with Evelyn and Alan in the Evangelical Covenant Church.

Debbie's nineteen years of ministry included teaching, training, and consulting in adult ministry, with emphasis on a wholistic approach addressing justice issues, in both the local church and seminary.

In reaching that "magical age," compensated ministry came to a close, but her call to serve the kingdom continued with renewed enthusiasm.

Debbie's current interests and activities have found her together on the team once again with Evelyn and Alan, giving attention to Boomers and beyond. She is finding new purpose in the new season of life where she finds herself these days. With more free time, Debbie, is now more available to serve in volunteer roles at her local church and provide spiritual direction.

A lifelong resident of Chicago, Illinois she raised three beautiful children who—in turn—added nine high-spirited grandchildren to the family.

Reji Laberje

Also working with Evelyn and Alan to create this vital story, was Independent Writing Mentor and Celebrity Co-author, Reji Laberje, of *Bucket List to Bookshelf*, a creative writing services company focused on a better world through better words. She has more than twenty years working in all aspects of the writing industry, including as founder of the successful publishing company she sold in 2017 (today called *Nico 11 Publishing & Design*). Her books include those co-written with Dick Vitale and Bob Brenner amongst more than a dozen positivity endorsers seeking relational writing experiences that honor their voices and stories. In addition, she has solo-written accomplishments across many genres including six children's books from #1 National Sports Publisher, Triumph Books. Reji has seven #1 Bestsellers in her more than forty books and plays and she looks forward to continuing in her passion for words all the days of her life.

Reji is a multi-lingual former Arabic linguist of the U.S. Air Force with a degree in international communications. She has a close family including two amazing sisters, many nieces, vitally-engaged parents, and blessed relationships around the nation and world. Today, Reji proudly lives and serves in her community in Wisconsin alongside her husband, son, daughters, daughter-in-law, and church family.

Learn more at: www.bucketlisttobookshelf.com.

"TO GOD BE THE GLORY, GREAT THINGS HE HATH DONE..." AND, GREAT THINGS HE IS DOING AND WILL DO....

ARE YOU READY FOR A CRESCENDO?

*As a Boomer who has just entered the world of retirement, I am already experiencing some of the losses related to aging. My challenge is to embrace the process of aging and to discover how I can continue to use the gifts and abilities God has given me. I want to be part of a church community that will encourage me to keep growing. **"Crescendo: An Ascent to Vital Living"** will equip church leaders (and individuals) to plan for those later years—and to create effective ministries for, by, and with older adults.*

~Millie Lungren
Served as Director of the Covenant Resource Center,
Associate Director of Adult Ministries
Evangelical Covenant Church

***"Crescendo: An Ascent to Vital Living"** is a compelling and thoughtful guide to planning ministries for older adults and to guide Boomers through their next phase of life. This is a go-to book for church leaders who want to effectively minister to the sixty-five and older age group.*

~Terri Cunliffe
President, Covenant Retirement Communities

As someone who pastors a church that is intentionally multi-generational, I have been searching for some help to engage and mobilize older adults. This is that book. There are real life stories that are very helpful in offering practical insights for ministry to and with people who are thinking about retiring or have already retired. We have many senior adults who have had successful careers and life experiences and now are looking for significance in their retirement years. Reading this book has challenged us to not settle for just potlucks and bus trips for seniors, but to utilize their life experience for vital ministry purposes.

Michael White
Pastor, Harbor Covenant Church
Gig Harbor, Washington

I am excited that Alan Forsman and Evelyn Johnson are providing this resource, **"Crescendo: An Ascent to Vital Living"**, for churches to explore the opportunities and challenges for ministry to older adults! Alan is a skillful communicator and he is passionate about helping churches and individuals to engage in visioning and planning. I know that his expertise and experience, together with that of Evelyn Johnson, will provide inspiration and practical ideas for Christians seeking to minister to the exploding population of older adults in our communities.

~Elsa Cisar
Divisional Social Services Director,
The Salvation Army - Del Oro Division

*With aging demographics and increased longevity, preparing church leaders and Boomers, themselves, for a Third Stage in life becomes a very pressing need for churches, their leaders, and for individuals. Evelyn and Alan are well prepared to provide guidance to this generation of which they are members. I look forward to implementing the advice of **"Crescendo: An Ascent to Vital Living"** in my own post retirement life.*

~Dr. Dean Lundgren
Served as Chief Financial Officer, Evangelical Covenant Church

*Evelyn Johnson and Alan Forsman are gifted leaders, teachers, and facilitators in both the church and nonprofit sectors. They both bring a unique blend of practitioner based wisdom and highly-skilled process and plan implementation. **"Crescendo: An Ascent to Vital Living"** is a timely book that will help the church leverage the significant demographic and generational shift towards greater Missional endeavor.*

~Dr. David W. Kersten
Dean, North Park Theological Seminary

As the world around us experiences rapid change, the wisdom, savvy, and spiritual maturity of older members of the Christian community is desperately needed by its younger members. I know of no better guides to help animate and unleash this potential than Evelyn Johnson and Alan Forsman.

~Dr. David P. Nystrom
Professor in Residence, Western Seminary Campus
Author of five books including: "James in the NIV," Application Commentary Series, and "History of Christianity"

Evelyn Johnson and Alan Forsman have been a formidable team for decades. When you combine their brilliance with their practicality, you can be sure that the result will be transformational. When their attention is focused on the church, especially the most significant growing edge of the church, you have a book like **"Crescendo: An Ascent to Vital Living".** *It is nothing short of a must read for those organizations that want to stay on the cutting edge of significant and eternal ministry that will make an impact for generations.*

~Kreig Gammelgard
Associate Superintendant, Director of Congregational Vitality
East Coast Conference

I would trust Evelyn and Alan to work with any church on any topic. I particularly trust Alan and Evelyn to help release the untapped and latent potential trapped in the Boomer and older generations.

~Dr. John Jackson President of William Jessup University
Author of "High Impact Church Planting"
and other Pastoral Resources

NOTES

NOTES